MW01681417

ELLI ROSE CIKOVIC

THE DIARY OF A TWENTY FIVE YEAR-OLD ALCOHOLIC

Copyright © 2025 by Elli Rose Cikovic
All rights reserved. Published by Cikovic Enterprises.

No part of this book may be reproduced, stored in a retrieval system, or transmitted in any form or by any means — electronic, mechanical, photocopying, recording, or otherwise — without prior written permission of the author or publisher, except as permitted by U.S. copyright law.

This work is a personal account of the author's experiences and reflections. It is intended to share honest insights about the subject matter covered, but it is not a substitute for legal, medical, financial, or other professional advice. Neither the author nor the publisher is engaged in rendering professional services of any kind. While every effort has been made to present this story responsibly, no representations or warranties are made regarding the accuracy, completeness, or applicability of the content. The strategies, practices, and choices described here worked for the author, but may not be appropriate for all readers. You should always consult a qualified professional regarding your own circumstances. Neither the publisher nor the author shall be liable for any loss, injury, or damages — including, but not limited to, special, incidental, consequential, personal, or commercial damages — arising from the use of or reliance on this material.

Disclaimer
This book is a memoir. It reflects the author's personal experiences, memories, and interpretations. Some names and identifying details have been changed to protect privacy. References to institutions, employers, and organizations — including colleges and universities — are included for context only. They are not affiliated with, nor do they endorse, this work. Any opinions expressed are solely those of the author.

ISBN: 979-8-218-82081-7

Book Cover Design: Olayemi Bolaji
Author Photograph: Fiona Rae Anderson
Illustration ("Alcoholic Monster"): Hannah Alston

Printed in the United States of America

A journey through my first two years of being alcohol-free and all the wild, sometimes unsafe situations that got me here.

There was **zero** AI used in the writing and editing of this book.
This is a *diary* for fuck's sake.

(Well, a unique version of a diary — bear with me.)

Dedicated to all my fellow alcoholics.

I love you.

A Quick Note (2025)

This book was written from May 24th, 2022, to May 24th, 2024, followed by a little over a year of editing. Throughout this book I talk highly (no pun intended) about using weed and shrooms during my first few years of being alcohol-free. However, prior to publishing in 2025, I made the decision to cut all recreational drug use from my life and to go fully *sober.*

This is not a space for judgement. This is just an honest story about my path to sobriety. We can choose to rewrite our stories every day. We can choose to change every day.

I have changed.
And I continue to change.
I love you and thank you for reading. Now, here we go...

Traded in wine for kombucha & weed for spices.
I love this new me.

PREFACE

I quit drinking on May 4th, 2022. Then, twenty days later, while I was sitting at my desk working for a professional basketball team in Atlanta, I started to write.

This book has become my lifeline. It is a living and breathing *thing*. It is a part of me. I think about it constantly. And the first draft was written fully on my iPad with a keyboard that lost a few buttons along the way. Impressive, right?

Well, my thoughts were suffocating me. I *needed* to get them out. And it has truly been the greatest release in the world to let them all go. Doing so has helped me process them. Sure, I am still working through these (which seem endless) feelings, but this book has helped me do it in a *healthy* way. It has also helped me with my communication skills around alcohol addiction, which is already challenging given the nature.

In the end, writing has set the foundation for me to develop into the woman who would one day be bold enough to release it all. So, no matter what happens with this book, my goal has always been simple... to help at least one person who might be struggling. And dear reader, I hope that person is *you*.

Okay, time for the theme song.

Queue "Bodies" by Jazmine Sullivan.

Contents

INTRODUCTION

Hi, my name is Elli and I am here to tell you a story. Well, many stories, and to provide you with some very valuable information that has helped me get to a massive turning point in my human existence thus far. I am talking about the point of finally being able to put down the one thing that had total control over me for the last ten years — *alcohol*. From ages fourteen to twenty-five, I lived in a constant state of anxiety and depression because of what my therapist calls my "binge drinking disorder."

Before I dive in, I need to be clear that this is not me telling you why you should quit drinking. This actually has nothing to do with you. If this book helps, great. If it makes you laugh, great. If it makes you want to grab a drink and be on the way to a blackout, sure, by all means, do as you please.

This book was simply written to tell you about *my* journey to alcohol sobriety and how all the wild, sometimes unsafe, and overall terrifying times got me to the point of being able to completely turn my life around at the age of twenty-five. If you decide to move forward, enjoy. And please, if you are here to judge, do it quietly. Actually... I don't really care. Fuck it. Here we go.

I was thirteen when I had my first drink. It was a combination of Captain Morgan and SunnyD stolen out of the bottom drawer of my oldest brother's dresser. The majority of the alcohol I consumed early on was stolen. I became a pro in high school at refilling the bottles in my father's liquor cabinet. Well, a semi pro, my dad usually ended up blaming my younger stepbrother for it. Let me make things clear — I was never perfect.

My first blackout was at the age of fourteen in a male friend's basement. Those nights seemed like they were playing on a constant loop for years. While I am not fully sure regarding the medical dangers of blacking out every weekend, I can promise you that the mental damage is enough to make you feel like you have been fucked by the devil himself. And I'm pretty sure there is some brain damage mixed in there as well.

There is nothing I would take back from my past. Did I make mistakes? Fuck ya. However, today, I am proud of how far I have come and I wouldn't be me without all the stupid shit I did.

It was the Wednesday after my twenty-fifth birthday when I officially decided to quit. I dreamt of that day for years, always thinking it would be when I had kids or something, you know, some sort of real ass responsibility other than myself and Buns (we'll get to her). Instead, something incredibly strong came over me. Something I hadn't felt before. I am still trying to process the feeling. I don't know how to explain it as anything other than a massive sigh of relief — it was time.

I am proud and a little bit confused about how I survived keeping good grades, getting good jobs, and maintaining powerful, loving friendships. I like to think that I managed my addiction externally pretty well, given the circumstances. However, internally, that's a whole different ball game. Okay, well, enjoy this glimpse into my life and I hope you can find something in it for you.

A Message to Myself:

What if it all works out? This book, acting, the dream. What if it all comes true? What if I become everything that I have dreamt of becoming? Role model, actor, author... what if it all really works out? Through all the pain, all the self-doubt, all the anxiety, all the stress, and all the *mistakes*... what if it all really works out?

I like to believe that it will.

1

My Story

Okay, let me give you a quick breakdown regarding pretty much everything about my life. I was born in Pittsburgh, Pennsylvania on April 27th, 1997, which makes me first year Gen Z (fuck ya). I am twenty-five, single, and living in Atlanta, GA as I write this. My daughter was born on July 11th, 2020. Her name is Buns, short for Oreo Bunny Cikovic — and yes, she is a bunny.

My three brothers (two blood, one step) and I went to high school about twenty minutes outside of the city of Pittsburgh in the good ole suburbs. Fortunately, I escaped when I was eighteen and moved across the country to attend Colorado State University. After college graduation, I moved to Atlanta to work for a professional basketball team in the sales department where I grew into quite the young professional. Within two years, I worked my way up to a Premium Account Executive which opened doors for me to meet a lot of amazing people — especially at the games. I am forever grateful for my experiences there, I learned a lot, and most importantly... I quit drinking while I was there.

Now, I work in remote tech sales from the comfort of my 21st floor home office. Sure, I eventually plan on being a full-time entrepreneur as an actor, writer, and businesswomen. But for now, this will just have to do to make a living. (If only I were a nepo baby, ugh.)

I am a Taurus, and Taurus is ruled by the planet Venus, which is the planet of love, beauty, and pleasure. My rising sign is Virgo and my moon sign is Capricorn, which makes me a triple Earth sign (slay). I am 5'5" but have always felt at least 5'7", I have a passion for Pure Barre workouts, and my favorite color is Olive Green because it reminds me of what I love most — mutha fuckin' nature baby.

When I was in the seventh grade all my friends came together to buy me a 6-foot Lil Wayne Fathead, which was taller than the real one to be exact. I have always loved Lil Wayne and I *loved* having him hanging up in my room. He played a crucial role in my taste for music and I know almost every word on his mixtape, *No Ceilings*. I grew up listening to R&B and Hip-hop because of my mom. Our car rides consisted of endless hours of Usher, Nelly, 50 Cent, Mariah Carey, Maxwell, Ja Rule, and more, which undoubtedly contributed to my taste in music today.

My parents got divorced when I was four years old, so most of my childhood was spent traveling back and forth between my mom's house and dad's house. I basically lived out of a Vera Bradley duffle bag those years. When I got to college, I remember feeling like I *finally* had my own space. That dorm room felt like the first place I could call home. I did end up moving to my dad's full time for the last two years of high school because my mom was... we will get into that later. But still, nothing felt like home until I had a three-hundred square foot room to share with my new best friend from San Diego, California.

My childhood was lonely to say the least, or as I like to call it "self-guided." No one has had a perfect childhood. I want to be clear about that. But mine always felt extra lonely, especially after my mom lost her house. My dad and stepmom tried their "best" to be there, but with full-time jobs in the city and multiple rental properties in Upstate New York, they were working nonstop. When I was younger, they would make us travel with them to the houses in NY almost every weekend, meaning I was drywalling and painting by age eleven. However, once I was "old enough" to stay at home, they would leave my younger stepbrother and me alone over the weekends. Which meant we had the house to ourselves... a recipe for disaster.

My older brothers were around, but they had their own lives in the city while attending the University of Pittsburgh. I like to think that everyone was doing their best, but still, it was hard. Especially those last two years of high school. I would never want to go back to that time. Those were the *worst* two years of my life.

When I started drinking, near the end of middle school, my oldest brother was a senior in high school. My mom still had her house at that time and would let him throw parties for his friend group. So, I was the little sober sister in the basement with all the older boys and girls partying, or at least I was sober at first. The alcohol was all there, readily available. What else could you expect from me? I have always been a curious little gal!

After my mom lost her house, that meant I couldn't have any of the parties like my brother did, which meant I had to find somewhere else to drink. With that original baseline conditioning, I was **always** going to find a basement with unlimited alcohol to party in. Or maybe it was always going to find me... destiny much? My high school experience consisted of *a lot* of underage drinking.

College in Colorado was nowhere close to a sober experience but moving to a state where I didn't know a single person, and a single person didn't know me, was the greatest thing I could have ever done for myself. Some may consider it running, but I look at it as finding myself. Sure, I was still severely depressed while living there, and my drinking was at an all-time high, but at least I was free from my childhood trauma... or so I thought.

I would never trash my college experience, it had its pros, but it was definitely not the "best four years of my life." Some of my strongest friendships to this day were formed while in college. I got a decent education, and I even worked for the football team as a recruiter all four years. It wasn't all bad, but the drinking sure was. I have always been able to keep good grades while partying *hard*, which turned out to be a blessing and a curse. Why? Because, on paper I looked like I was doing great, however, mental success is very different. I was incredibly depressed the entire time I was in Colorado. That is where I learned that memories stick, no matter how far you try to run.

I met my first serious "adult" boyfriend the summer before my senior year of college. He made me happy. We maintained a long-distance relationship for about a year until I graduated, and then we both moved into a small house on the Southwest Side of Atlanta with two of his close friends. Living in that house turned out to be a... very developmental time of my life. During that time, I (for some reason) decided to go off of my antidepressants. And so, with a combination of my unstable mental condition, one of the roommates getting a girl pregnant and moving her in, and the other roommate moving in *another* random girl from Australia... made for a very unhappy Elli in a *complex* living situation. There were six of us in a three-bedroom house. Oh wait, there was also a person living in the basement, so seven. Things were tight. And then to make matters even worse, COVID-19 hit and we could not leave the house. This was when I began having *at least* a bottle of wine a day.

But again, it wasn't all bad. We had some great times in that house. I also learned (the hard way) how badly I need my own space to be a functioning human being in society. Fuck, I almost lost my god damn mind being around that many people *all the time*. I grew up alone, so I need space to be alone. Simple as that.

My boyfriend (ex) and I ended up moving out a year later into a one-bedroom apartment in Midtown, Atlanta. I finally got some of my "alone" time back. And then, a few months (and a bunny) later, I was living completely alone. Which also meant — drinking alone.

Living alone gets lonely, but I have found myself during this time of solitude. I became an actor during this time. I became a writer during this time. I quit drinking during this time — and quitting drinking is the greatest thing I have ever done for myself. For me, quitting was the true definition of self-love. So ya, I have a lot that I want to share about my journey to alcohol sobriety, and most importantly, *why*.

P.S. This is my first time writing a book and I have no idea what I am doing. So please, bear with me. I just *need* to share my story. I also believe that there are a lot of women, men, or however you identify, that can relate and hopefully learn a thing or two from my mistakes. If that is you, I hope my story can save you some time on your own journey. Alcohol is not for everyone, especially not for people like me, and I think it's time that we all talk about *why.*

And hey, trauma always leads to a good story, right?

2

So, Why Did I Quit?

How can I best explain to people, who do not know me on a personal level, the reason why I quit drinking alcohol? Why should anyone care? Will this even make sense? Truth is, I ask myself these questions on the daily, and what I consistently hear back is:

"Fuck it Elli, the truth will come out. Just keep typing."

And somehow, it has turned into something pretty magical. I know this book will help people. So here I am, telling my story with no incentives other than knowing that this is what I am meant to do. I have an opportunity to empower thousands, hopefully millions, of people struggling with alcohol use in their daily lives, and to possibly make a change. How could I not at least try?

So again, why did I quit drinking? That is the question at hand. It is also why I have spent years now writing this unorganized "book" of thoughts and ideas to hopefully figure that out myself. And somehow, I still have not been able to simplify it down to one, simple sentence as to *why*.

Was it the non-stop hangovers and vomiting? Was it the countless nights of unwanted sexual experiences? Was it the longline of family history with addiction and depression? I still don't know. What I do know though is that the day I quit, was the day I finally *needed* to. No further explanation necessary, really.

But fuck it, let me write a book.

Over the last two years of being alcohol-free, I have learned quite a lot about myself and my family history. I come from Pittsburgh, a city built on steel-workers and beer. Both of my parents grew up in small towns in the middle of butt-fuck nowhere Pennsylvania. My dad is the baby of ten siblings and was raised on a dairy farm near Hershey, PA. This side of my linage comes from an extensive line of Croatian farmers. My mom's side comes from another small redneck Pennsylvania town where the Amish live next door. Think Punxsutawney Phil. She is the opposite of a redneck, so that alone gave her enough childhood trauma to rely on the bottom of a bottle. Both of my parents fortunately escaped their small towns and worked hard to break generational curses. They both obtained college educations from the University of Pittsburgh, where they met and eventually gave birth to me and my two brothers.

A lot happened during my childhood that led me to heavy binge-drinking. We all experience childhood trauma. It is a fact. Yes, some cases are more extreme than others, but everything is just a scale, really, if you are *comparing*. I choose to not compare my life experiences to others on a scale of "who had it worse" because if you really take the time to hear what some of the people around you have gone through, you will quickly learn that we have all dealt with (and are still dealing with) the same sort of shit. Everyone fucking struggles, and that is okay.

So, maybe I quit because I was sick of struggling more than I needed to. I *had* to quit. That is the thing about quitting something, you just have to do it. Nothing anyone else says or does will get you to quit besides yourself. You just gotta do it. That's it. Simple right? Well, no, not really. It took me years of mistakes to get to the point of quitting. Years of trying to go at least 72 hours without drinking. Years of failing.

When I had my last drink, I did not know it would be just that. It was a glass of wine at a friend's house, a friend who opted out on having a glass with me. She was okay being sober while I sat there and drank *her* wine alone on *her* couch.

The concept of not drinking in this type of situation was foreign to me. But that decision of hers sparked something in me. After that night I decided to try another 72-hour cleanse, and on about hour 48 when I woke up, something felt different. I looked in the mirror and saw someone different. Someone ready to start living.

It is hard to put the exact feeling into words, but I will try to do just that. When I woke up that morning the thought of taking another sip of alcohol sounded like the most disgusting thing in the world, and to this day, I have not lost that feeling. I could never imagine taking another sip.

Not everyone drinks how I did. Once I start, I cannot stop. It is a vampire blood thirst that can only end in blackout and regret. Alcohol is a form of self-harm for me and I continued to drink it because I thought it was my only choice to feel better. To me, alcohol is poison, and there is no happy medium with consumption. I had absolutely no control over the things I did when I would go dark. I tried so many times to become a "good drinker," aka not blacking out every single time, but always failed. After nights that I didn't blackout, I would wake up and be so proud of myself.

There are hundreds of hours that I do not remember living. I have walked, talked, fucked — you name it — all over this country, well multiple countries to be exact, completely blacked out. My drinking was at an all-time high when I lived in Europe for six months in 2018. I went out and partied one-hundred days in a row. *One-fucking-hundred*. I will cover more on my times in Europe later, but there was definitely a guardian angel watching over me during that time because I did not give a flying fuck whether I lived or died. I truly cannot believe I came home in one piece.

For ten years, my days were spent looking for the next event to be able to drink and escape my mind. It ruled everything in my life: friend groups, activities, sex, work, and even... my bathroom schedule. I justified everything I did because of age and adolescence, when deep down I knew that I had a problem. I was just not ready to admit that yet.

I do not wish to take back any of the time or experiences I had over the last ten years, but I am really fucking grateful they are over. Today, I feel true happiness.

My experiences of waking up with shame and regret needing someone to tell me what happened, how I got home, or trying to figure out why my underwear are in my purse, with no idea how they got there, are *over.*

Throughout this book I am going to tell you about the mindset I developed and the experiences I had that finally got me to the point of looking in the mirror and saying, "Fuck you, alcohol. I am done." I have about ten years of damage in a box that I need to open up and process, and I would like to take you along with me. Writing this book has saved me. I do not remember half of the nights or half of the people that have had access to my body, but through this book I plan to take my power back — day by day. I have a better set of tools now, and they work. They really fucking work.

Also, I would be lying if I didn't say discovering my spirituality was a major turning point in my life to help me quit drinking. I incorporate crystals, plant medicine, and tarot cards in my daily life now. So yes, I am one of those girls.

My story is like millions who live in their trauma on a day-to-day basis, drinking into the abyss of nonexistence. We wear it like a blanket, a weak set of armor that only adds on layers upon layers of trauma and weak defenses. For example, "I feel sad about my relationship with my dad. Let me drink so I don't feel so sad about that, and then when I wake up, I can be sad because I blacked out and fought with my roommate." Like I said, a very shitty blanket.

Only now do I realize how sick I was. I would transcend into the darkest depths of blackout kingdom. The alcoholic monster and I were best buds. (Not in a good way.)

And like I mentioned before, the purpose of this book is not to tell you why you should quit drinking. This is just me, telling my story. Not everyone struggles with alcoholism or a binge drinking disorder like me, *but everyone knows someone that does.*

Now, onto the first story.

3

My First Blackout

To set the scene... it's 2011, I am fourteen, a freshman in high school, and my two best friends and I had just covered up my life size barbie doll with blankets and pillows to make it look like three teenage girls sleeping peacefully. Let me tell ya, this set up was not fooling anyone. I'm not sure how I got away with some of this shit I did back then, but thank god I wasn't a teenager when Ring cameras came out. No, this was 2011, and we got away with sneaking out — often.

After patiently waiting for my dad and stepmom to fall asleep, we "quietly" snuck out the back door and ran through the cold wet grass to a basement located just up the street.

Ahh... wet grass, 60-degree weather, and basements that smell like Blue Wave and Bud Light. Now that is the smell of my Pennsylvania, baby! Sometimes I miss those days. It's weird. It's more like nostalgia. Anyways, back to the basement. This guy had a big house with a big basement and a mother that didn't check up on him, a perfect underage drinking environment.

I was part of the high school friend group that partied and drank — a lot. We were the "fucked-up freshmen," then moved on to the "sloppy sophomores," and so on. These labels weren't technically wrong, but let me tell ya, it was not fun walking into school every Monday morning just to find out about some crazy and embarrassing shit I did over the weekend while sitting in Spanish 1.

But okay, back to my first blackout night. It was my two girlfriends, myself, and six or seven guys, good guys, who I considered to be friends. We all had early stage drinking problems, most still do (no offense y'all). Over the course of this specific fall night, we played plenty of drinking games. Games that weren't really "games," but just ways for us to pass around the handle of Blue Wave and drink enough until we vomited out our insides. Have you ever heard of Thunder, Kings Cup, or just simply pouring vodka into a bong and taking it to the face? If not, good for you.

The guy hosting the party was dating a friend of mine who was not present at this get-together. And unfortunately, when I woke up the next morning, miraculously on my basement floor, I found out that I had made out with him. The last thing I remembered was being on the couch in his basement and this massive array of different lights and movements that came over me and then... nothing. This first blackout was confusing. I didn't understand what happened and had no one to talk to about it. I just remember feeling this strong underlying *guilt* and confusion, and this feeling didn't go away for the next ten years.

This was the first time I had done something to hurt someone without knowing it. This right here is a perfect example of why I am telling my story. This feeling... it was so shitty. And it was not the last time I did something like this, but it was the first. To put it in perspective, this was only my second time heavily drinking. My first time, I had a few shots and peed in my mother's sink. This time, I blacked out and made out with my friend's boyfriend. All my self-trust was lost that morning.

To have done something you would never do without the influence of alcohol should be enough to never drink again. But unfortunately, I didn't have this knowledge back then. Also, apologizing for something you don't remember doing is such an interesting feeling. Like, you can't feel fully sorry for what you did, because you don't remember it, but you do feel sorry for the situation you put that person in and that you let your problems create someone else's pain.

So, to all the women whose boyfriends, partners, husbands (fuck me) that I've hooked up with and do not remember over the last ten years, I am terribly sorry. Gosh, I was so young and damaged. Talk about character development from an early age. I wish I could give that version of myself a big hug. But I did more for her, I quit.

I really should have quit drinking after that first night. I wanted to, but *nope*. This was just the beginning of years of countless nights in basements with a handle of Blue Wave and drunk, horny boys. And don't even get me started on how interesting it got once the boys older brothers joined in... yikes. The older boys loved my friends and me. That is when I really learned how to drink. Junior parties were different than freshman parties, more advanced, and I was at almost every single one of them by the age of fourteen.

Vulnerable, no protection, and a hunger to feel the love and affection I was missing in other parts of my life. Safe to say that things got dark, but let's keep going.

4

The Breakdown

How It Started... I will never forget my first drink. Captain Morgan chased down with SunnyD. My best friend and I were in eighth grade at the time and had no idea what we were doing. That first tingling sensation was jolting, painful, and enjoyable — all at the same time. I enjoyed the feeling that I could be and feel different after one sip. In reality I was sober, considering we only had a few sips before gagging, but that feeling was freeing, and so there my curiosity started.

Depression was present early in my life and I have always felt the need to escape. I went to therapy for the first time when I was only four years old, right after the divorce. There were early signs of mental struggles, but the deep depression didn't come until after my first blackout. That is when I first met the other Elli. The Elli that does things out of her loneliness, abandonment, complicated family dynamic, and self-hatred.

When you're a kid, it's hard to comprehend how messed up your situation really is. For me, instead of focusing on my life at home, I focused all my attention on boys. Yes, boys. Fuck me. In my head, it was all about sex, relationships, and trying to feel "loved." Well, whatever version of love I thought existed at that time.

I have cried over so many boys in my life, and to be honest, most of them were... um... let me be nice here... fucking idiots. Sure, now that I am older and have matured, at least a little bit, I have come to realize that everyone struggles, especially as kids, so I am sure these boys had their own pains of being young men. But still, they could have done better. I have always been attracted to assholes.

As I look back on those years in high school, I realize now that I worked pretty hard to make problems for myself rather than focusing on my loneliness at home. I worked hard to make the biggest pain in my life boys not loving me enough or not wanting me enough, meanwhile, I would be passed out drunk in the corner of some random classmates basement. And who the fuck wants anything to do with that? That is self-sabotage at its finest. Alcohol mixed with depression, loneliness, and anxiety results in a horribly sad teenage girl. Damn do I wish I had more help and support back then.

The truth is that the real problems in my life had nothing to do with those boys. My problems were bigger, much bigger. But my lil ole head couldn't understand that quite yet, so we drank. We partied and we drank — a lot.

How It Continued... My worst blackouts were in college. My most horrific sex experiences were in college. A lot of my life's scariest moments were in college. This is not me saying that I didn't enjoy it. I created lifelong bonded friendships, and I guess I also benefited intellectually from the overpriced educational system. I learned to study others. I also learned about the importance of female friendship, so, of course it was a beautiful experience. However, I absolutely do not stand by college being for everyone nor it being a requirement to have a good life. College can be overwhelming and dangerous as hell if you are a heavy drinker. Especially if you are a young woman + heavy drinker + depressed + finally free from curfew. That combination will equate to many near death experiences.

Again, this is just me. I am not saying that drinking is always bad or that you are bad if you do it. Everyone is different, but alcohol is most definitely bad for *me*. I am grateful for my drinking years because it's how I met some of the most amazing people in my life, but those dark days are over. And I am happy about that.

So, why was my drinking so bad? For me: alcohol abuse = self-abuse.

How would you define alcoholism and binge drinking disorder? Personally, I look at it as a form of self-destruction, and in theory, a form of self-harming. At least to the levels I was using it. I was absolutely self-harming with alcohol. I cannot even count the number of days I spent on a bathroom floor throwing up stomach acid repeatedly until it felt like I was about to die. Alcohol poisoning was normal for me, especially in college.

The sicknesses never stopped me though because the second I felt somewhat better, I'd let myself do it all over again. I had to. I had to escape my head and my life. I had to escape my body, which I was so uncomfortable in. Every time I looked in the mirror, I hated myself, and the only thing that ever made me feel better was to drink more. Then once I started, I would not stop until everything went away, to a blackout, which would then lead to another day on the bathroom floor throwing up stomach acid. That yellow metal tasting substance became so familiar pouring out of my throat and sometimes it was as if that was the goal because then I would be able to spend a day laying there, lifeless. It felt good in a twisted way, even though it was physically painful beyond belief. But for some reason... I liked the pain.

I remember the first time I saw my mom throwing up from being too drunk. I was young, and this memory is blurry, but I swear I looked just like her every time I did it. I would always get so mad at her when she was like that, but it turns out I was just like her. Alcoholism is an inherited disease.

It blows my mind how some people can drink and not take it to the levels I did. There is a serious line between those with and without drinking disorders. I was killing my body every time, ripping my stomach (and heart) out. It was toxic for me.

However, I always found a way to make the drinking feel new and different. That's how I kept the abuse up without making it look like I had a real problem — different party, different season, different drink. I was able to manipulate my mind into believing I was exploring and growing, not hurting. However, now when I look back, all I was doing was hurting. I was so fucking hurt. So sad. So sick. *Hurting.*

The most nights (and days) that I do not remember are from when I was living abroad during my college junior year in Prague. I missed an entire bar crawl in Amsterdam on St. Patrick's Day because I was blacked out. Sure, I was there, but I don't remember a damn thing for at least eight hours. And unfortunately, this was a very common pattern in my life. Instead of experiencing my life, I would wake up with missing items, terrifying videos of me dancing like a zombie, angry friends, lost panties, and a daylong of throwing up stomach acid. That was my life, over and over, again and again.

Half of my life during my drinking years was spent waking up and having to rely on friends to tell me what I did the night before. I had such little control over my life, for so long. Do you know how hard it is for a highly anxious person to not know what, where, or how something happened? And to do that continuously? I was torturing myself. And all of those situations were interpreted by someone else, not me. I love my friends, but I was relying solely on them to tell me what I did during all of those long nights — friends who were also young and drunk. I had misinformation for so many years and reacted to things that were not necessarily true. We are all focused on ourselves and in our own heads, so no one was paying as much attention to me as I thought, therefore the information was jagged.

I felt such little control over my life and head for so long. If I could go back and see what was really happening during all those hours, I probably would have interpreted a lot of things completely different. Not that I want my life to be any different now, but maybe I could have had a little less anxiety, and that would have been nice.

How It Ended... Are memories better than the actual experience? I have been thinking back to all the drunk nights that we look back on and say, "Ah, what an amazing night!" But those nights were never as good as the "memories." I was never happy taking those shots or throwing up in some random frat boy's or club's bathroom. I created better memories in my head so that when I went to drink again, I had a reason to think this time could be an "amazing night" since the last time was "so much fun."

Lies. Lies, lies, and more lies.

Every time I had faith that I would not take it too far, I always did. It was an itch I could never scratch for a falsified feeling that was never good for me. It was abusive. And it was insanity.

There were many "final straws" that got me close to the point of quitting. But that one morning in particular, everything changed. I did not wake up that morning in May of 2022 thinking that it would be my last day of drinking forever — it just was.

I wake up every day now and choose myself. Without drinking, memories are the truth of the life I have made for myself, not some falsified alcohol lensed experience. I am no longer forcing or faking enjoyment and fun. Although the high adrenaline experiences are less often now, they are better. So much better. My life is better.

Drew Barrymore, who is now living an alcohol-free life, said it best, "I am never going to be that cool girl at the party with a glass of wine, like I will want three bottles. That is just my personality, it is my addiction." It really is as simple as that and I don't think that I can explain it any better. Drinking is not for me. It never was, and never will be.

Now onto the next story.

5

Two 14-Year-Old Blondes with Big Tits and A Bottle of Vodka

It was the summer after my freshman year of high school and I was living with my mom in an apartment complex where, luckily, my best friend was living too. This friend and I did everything together for years. However, *unluckily*, her mom announced she was getting remarried and they were set to move to Milwaukee by the end of the summer. I knew I was fucked once she moved. She was my best friend and no one else understood me like she did. She was my favorite person to do everything with. Then as a plus, we both loved to *party*.

Before her move, we had plans to go to Ocean City, Maryland with my mom's side of the family, and this particular beach trip ended up being very... memorable.

I loved bringing her on my family beach vacations. We both enjoyed walking on the boardwalk at night and getting hit on by all the boys (and old dudes). Talk about a confidence boost! One guy told me once that I looked like Celine Dion and I was pumped (he was at least sixty). What we also loved about the Ocean City, Maryland boardwalk was the 18 and under club. If any of you have heard of Club H20, then you know exactly what I am talking about. It is a "club" where horny and sweaty teenagers go to grind, dance, and make out — with a shit ton of underage drinking mixed in there as well. This was also before social media (besides Facebook) so we were able to be free and get *super frisky*. No one had their phones out 24/7 and damn do I really miss those days. Granted, I was only fourteen years old, so thank god no one saw what I was doing in there — but damn, we had some really great times in that club. We were two hot young blondes with no waists, D cup tits, and a bottle of blueberry vodka. What could go wrong!

One day while on the beach with my family, we met two hot guys and made plans to meet up with them later at the lifeguard stand before going to the club. They brought a water bottle full of Smirnoff Vodka... classic. We pregamed on the beach and paired up with the boy that each of us liked. *Apparently,* my guy and I made out on the lifeguard stand before we drunkenly took it to the dance floor in the club. I do not remember anything after getting to the dance floor, the lifeguard chair already being pretty blurry. The club's theme that night was *Foam Night*, so massive amounts of foam were falling from the ceiling onto this mosh pit of us horny teens, it was sick, and the music was always *amazing*. Oh, how I miss 2012 hits. I used to love to grind and jersey turnpike to songs like "Dance (A$$)," "Pop That," "Low," and "Shots," with no fucks given. And now that I think of it, I really had some dancing power back then. I was confident as hell. This is probably because I didn't get super depressed until this friend left Pittsburgh. This vacation is one of the last memories I have of things feeling *normal*. However, nothing about my behavior was normal. Next thing I remember was waking up in our shared bed at my family's rental and my mom was... pissed.

Apparently, I got so drunk that I threw up on the dance floor, we both lost our phones, and I passed out on the beach. My friend had to borrow a stranger's phone on the boardwalk to call my mom to come and get us. Once my mom and uncle arrived, *apparently*, they got me in the back seat of my uncle's car where I started to throw up again, everywhere... yikes. My mom recently told me that she and my uncle had to very skillfully sneak us back in the condo without my grandma seeing. My grandma is a very religious woman and she was also paying for the beach house, so it would have been very bad if she saw what was going on. Gosh, I wish I remembered at least a little bit from that night, but *nope*. And by the next day, no one ever spoke a single word about it again. My grandma still has no clue.

After we woke up, my friend and I set out on a mission to find our phones. We had lost them at some point throughout the night — most likely on the dance floor in the massive amount of foam — so our hopes were not high on finding them, but we were at least going to give it a try. This was back when iPhones were new and had barely any tracking features. However, they did have "Find My iPhone." I cannot tell you how many times "Find My iPhone" has saved my life (phone attachment is real). Literally almost every time I would blackout, I would lose my phone. It was a given. It even happened on the night of my last blackout, but I will save that story for later.

Back to the beach... we found a Verizon store on the boardwalk and the employees kindly let us use their computer to track the missing phones. Little did I know, one of my guy friends at school changed my iCloud name to "BIG FAT YUMMY DICKS" or something like that, so once the iPhone location popped up, so did the name. Those poor guys working just stared at me. It was so awkward and I looked a lot younger without my short shorts, pushup bra, and makeup on. I was a child. However, the angels of iPhone heaven must have loved us because our phone's locations popped right up to Club H20, baby! We bolted there. Two teenage girls without their phones were nothing. We needed them. I *needed* to know if that hot boy from the night before texted me or if I ruined everything by getting too drunk. *Spoiler alert*: I never heard from him again. This happened often over the next ten years to come.

We went to the front of the club and waited for someone to show up. It was 10 a.m. and we looked very distraught. However, at that age hangovers weren't terrible. They were much easier at fourteen than twenty-four. I can't even imagine what they would be like at thirty-four... good thing I will never have to find that out.

Once the owner showed up, thankfully, he took us to the back office, and just like *magic,* both of our phones were sitting face down on his desk. Mine had the cutest little brown camo case on it and I was so fucking excited to see that iPhone 4. However, the boy did not text me, and I was now sad. But it makes sense because we were fifteen and he just probably never saw a girl go that fucking hard before.

This trip was one of the last memories I have of my mom being a "mother" to me during my childhood, aka having the ability to punish me. We were "grounded" the rest of the trip. Okay, my mom's version of grounding was literally a side eye, but it still affected me.

Looking back, I wish I knew how dangerous blacking out could be. During this time I was still a virgin and not letting boys touch me, other than making out and jersey turnpiking (loved that shit). I had about a year and a half to go until the full body guilt after a blackout would start. Sex made drinking more dangerous, it opened a whole other level of darkness in me. This was a kinder time. I still had my mom and my best friend, at least for a little. Things turned dark quickly after this summer and I had a lot of fucked up shit ahead of me. But at least now I can look back and hug that little girl and say, "I got you." Because I do.

6

Drinking in Moderation: A Myth… for me

A few people have suggested the idea that I could *monitor* my drinking one day. You know, be a cute, cool, and modest drinker. Like maybe one to two glasses of wine every few days, a fun drink while out with friends, or *occasionally* a shot. That sounds nice, but there is just no fucking way.

I will never be a moderate drinker. It's just not… possible. Let me be clear, it is not just the physical "in the moment" act of drinking for me. It is that little voice in my head that will start to slowly think about the next drink more and more, and then ever so swiftly, I am scheduling my entire day around how I can get it. Then I am right back into the constant loop of, "When is the next drink?" "Did I do okay with that drink?" and "Oh shit, what happened?" It is overwhelming to even think about.

Drinking was always an "all or nothing" thing for me. I am not sure how else to describe it. Alcoholism is an allergy, as I learned in the single AA meeting I attended. And truthfully, I am scared as shit of it. I don't trust myself when I drink. I fear myself because I cannot handle it. It controls me. And I am honestly a little tired of people trying to make it seem like this is something someone with this disease can just turn off and on one day. It is not possible. And it sucks.

Have you ever seen *The Vampire Diaries*? You know how Stephan would turn his feelings off? And just go fucking crazy? For those of y'all that don't know what I am talking about, basically Stephan was a vampire that refused to drink human blood unless he... turned off his feelings. And when he would decide to do so (because vampires can), he would immediately kill and drink the blood of like 200 people within an hour timespan. He just couldn't control it. That's exactly what happens when I let myself have "just one drink." Okay, maybe I am being dramatic — I tend to do that. And damn I wish I were a vampire. But really, it is never just one drink. It is "just one drink" and then just another and then just another and then it's every fucking night and then I am back in a full-blown loop of self-medicating and destruction. It just doesn't work, and I don't want it to work. I don't want to drink. I don't want to be controlled again. And then there is also the fact that alcohol is just not good for you. Like it really is not fucking good for you.

I have finally gotten to the point where I don't get bothered by people mentioning this idea of "monitoring my drinking." They just want to help. The answer is still absolutely not, but I don't say it so aggressively anymore. During my first year of alcohol sobriety, my initial reaction was to get defensive. I would get so protective of this thing. This *thing* I created. This version of myself that I am now identifying with, or sometimes as. Really, I don't want to identify with this *thing*, aka a sober person (minus plant medicine — we will get to that), but honestly, I kind of have to. How can I not? I am writing this damn book, aren't I? And drinking was the center of my life for so long. When someone makes that drastic of a change, their past self will always be with them. But it doesn't have to be a bad thing. I can still go out and dance with my friends with this *thing*. Sure, it may be awkward and uncomfortable at first, but it is so much better than having to call those friends the next morning to ask what happened or how I got home. Plus, I just had to accept the fact that drinking is so deeply rooted into our society that it will always be noticeable if I am the only one not doing it. Some things I have just had to accept, and that is okay.

Not drinking is simply a decision I made for myself because I love myself and I want to have a good and beautiful life. But it's still very hard. I won't lie about that. This is why I had to identify with it and make it a part of my personality. You have to at first, to survive being *sober*. I am still learning how to deal with it. And yes, sometimes it is hard to be around a bunch of people that I used to yell "shots" at to now being the only *sober* one in the room. Sometimes I catch people watching me and how I act in social situations when I am not drinking. I don't like the attention. Well, I tell myself this, but maybe I do like the attention. Why else am I writing this book?

Well, this book is my art, that's why I am writing it. Okay, hey, you are getting a literal insight into my brain, well, my diary... edited. I have edited this shit for sure.

But really, I am writing this book because I want to be truthful about my experiences. Truthful about my addiction with alcohol. Truthful about my mistakes. And truthful about the miraculous changes that have happened since the moment that I quit.

Fun fact: Alcohol alters your brain frequency.

Frequencies influence human emotions, behaviors, cognition, and overall physical well-being. I am not a doctor nor a scientist, this is self-research, and again... this is a diary.

During my last two years drinking I was having at least a bottle of wine a day, on average. Well, weekday. Thursday through Sunday meant unlimited drinking, so a bottle of wine was just the topper at the end of the night after mimosas, beer, shots, cocktails, maybe a combination of all-in-one cup, you name it. I would drink whatever alcohol I could get my hands on. Wine made it feel more acceptable, classier. Throwback to the time when Pineapple Burnetts ruled my life for a few good years. Nasty.

Basically, I became a pro at lowering my frequency because it made me feel better in the moment. When in actuality, it was doing the complete opposite.

Alcohol kept me at a low frequency. That's where it best operates. It is a depressant and triggers the receptors in your brain that can "switch off" elevated levels of brain activity. That is what alcohol does, it helps you "switch off," specifically the brain neurons. They become negatively charged brain cells, which means they are sitting there doing nothing, aka making you "relaxed."

However, brain cells do not just "switch off" without some kind of negative side effect. So, essentially, what the brain does when drinking a lot of alcohol over an extended period is it will try to remove as many "light switches" as possible, aka brain cells, so there are less to "turn off," aka it is KILLING YOUR BRAIN CELLS.

And what happens when you are not consuming alcohol? Your brain is in a constant frenzy looking for this mysterious chemical that turns the receptors off, because without the constant alcohol, they have nowhere to go, therefore causing things like anxiety, insomnia, depression, and even seizures for the heavier drinkers. Your brain forms a need for this chemical to shut the receptors off and keep you in a negative charge. Does this sound fun to you?

Again, I am not a scientist nor a doctor, but from my own personal research — this shit is crazy. And that is only a snippet into the effects that alcohol has on your brain. So, why do so many of us continue to feed ourselves this harmful and addictive substance? Well, there are a lot of reasons, and at the end of the day all of this information is just *information*. It's what you decide to do with the information that counts.

P.S. The number of times that I blacked out and fully disassociated at such an early age was... *concerning*. I was fully "living" in my trauma and pain. I don't miss those nights anymore, but I did for a while when I first quit. I missed the "easy escape" from my pain. So, if you are just starting to quit, be easy on yourself. It's okay to miss your abuser at first. But I promise you, it will get easier to walk away. Just takes a lil' bit of work.

7

Killian's Basement

I was fifteen when I got in trouble with the police for the first time for underage drinking. But before we get into that, I need to start off by telling you about someone that holds a very special place in my heart. Killian Cavanaugh was one of the most intelligent and talented human beings that I had the honor of knowing and loving for so many years. Killian and his family played a major role in my life throughout my middle school and high school days, specifically ages thirteen to sixteen. I spent almost every weekend at his house during that time. His mom was basically my second mom, and she provided me with a lot of knowledge at an early age.

Killian showed me how to be confident in my crazy and wild self, because he sure as hell was. We made countless YouTube videos of us dancing to songs like "My Humps" and "Bicycle Race" — the kid had *range.* We would jump in the snow in our bathing suits and compete for who could stay out the longest. We spent hours ding-dong ditching and really just causing overall destruction to the local neighborhoods. We traveled hours around Western Pennsylvania and Ohio to different haunted houses every fall, all in his moms Range Rover of course. We were *crazy* everywhere that we went. I experienced a lot with Killian, it almost feels like my entire childhood was spent with him, the good years at least. And then of course, we experienced getting our first MIPs (minor in possession) together.

All of our fun was innocent at first, but once high school rolled around, we started to get drunk. Super fucking drunk. I spent most of my freshman and sophomore year weekends drinking in Killian's basement. The parties started out small with just a few of us... but eventually they turned into massive gatherings with kids coming from all over Pittsburgh. His parents were always upstairs, and most other parents (including mine) knew what was going down at Killian's. I guess we all assumed it was a "safe" environment. And Killian's mom would usually try to stop things before they ever got out of hand. However, things did get a little too rowdy one night. Story time.

The First Underage

It was my sophomore year of high school and we were at one of Killian's famous basement parties. He had transferred to a private school our freshman year which resulted in him meeting a lot of kids from all over the city. The turnouts were crazy, and we partied hard in that basement. I am grateful for those nights because it was under the roof of people that I loved and trusted. I always felt safe and comfortable there, maybe even a little too comfortable.

The night ended up getting pretty blurry for me, *per usual*, and about halfway through the party I remember hearing a bunch of screams and then everyone starting to run. Turns out a girl in the grade above got too drunk and had vicious alcohol poisoning in the bathroom and Killian's mom had to call an ambulance... which also meant the cops.

I remember running upstairs frantically and then being in the foyer with my friend Bella who was trying to get me to escape. She was like, "Come on Elli, come home with me!" But then here came Killian out of the corner of my eye and he grabbed me and took me outside. Sorry Bella! At this point, it was clear that the police were coming, but I was drunk and didn't seem to comprehend the severity of that, so I said, "Fuck it, let's ride!" My dumbass thought escaping the house with the boy that lived there made sense. Like what was I thinking. No way he would get away. But I guess when I was that drunk it didn't matter, I trusted him, and so together we went. The police were pulling up in the driveway when Killian and I ran out the front door. I remember seeing the lights and hearing the police yelling, "STOP!" One girl ran for the woods and Killian and I jumped in the nearest bush. Neither of us thought we were visible but turns out we were just stupid. I remember hearing the police officer saying, "Where did he go?" And then Killian's ass poked his head up out of the bush to look, and then immediately popped right back down. The officer then yelled, "Get out of the damn bush!" Killian yelled back, "Fine!" and looked back at me and said, "Come on Elli!" As if it was exciting. Gosh, everything was exciting to him. The officers made us get out of the bush and walk shamefully back into the house.

So, there were seven of us lined up on the couch and we all had to call our parents to come get us. At this point, my mom was going through her own shit, but she was still a better call than my dad. Once the parents got there, it was time for the breathalyzer and I was set to go last. Some time passed and then once it was my turn, the officer looked at me after I blew, smiled, and said "Congrats!" And I was like, "Omg what!" And then he was like, "You blew the highest!" Fucking asshole. My mom told me the next day that I was, *apparently*, drunk talking to the TV while watching the Pirates game and at one point I looked at the police officer when he was breathalyzing the others and yelled, "I love baseball!" right at him and then looked straight back to the TV. Drunk Elli was funny... I'll give her that. Also, I hate baseball.

After this night, I was grounded. My dad was *pissed*.

A few weeks later we had our court date. So yeah, picture seven teenagers with their parents sitting in a small county court room — we were *all* getting scolded by the judge. I guess it was kind of funny, but not really. Everyone with a license got a six-month suspension, but since Killian and I were so young, only our permits were suspended. All charges were dropped too. Guess it was a good thing that Killian's dad is a lawyer.

A *fun fact* I learned after this night is that while the seven of us were downstairs getting MIP's, there were at least 20-30 kids hiding upstairs in multiple closets. For hours. Adolescent stupidity at its finest.

Writing this story makes me miss those nights. It makes me miss Killian. Some of my favorite memories were with him and his family. We grew up together.

Killian was a brother to me. He was the kind of kid that dressed up as Justin Bieber and sang in the look-alike competition at Ross Park Mall for fun. Really, he was just a genius theatre kid disguised as a Justin Bieber wannabe. He also drew the most beautiful pictures, one of Heath Ledger as the Joker, which is still my favorite to this day. And he read books the size of his head. I admired him.

Killian passed away on December 9th, 2017, at the age of 20. That was an awful day.

I was driving home from a beach trip about sixteen months into my alcohol-sobriety and I swear I looked up in the sky and could hear Killian saying, "I am proud of you." I just cried. Killian saw first-hand that I had serious issues with alcohol (and men) at a young age. He saw my self-destructive tendencies, often. Killian wasn't the type of guy to get too drunk, he was always alert. He saw the pain I was trying to mask. He was wise but never made me feel judged. And sometimes that's all that someone in pain needs — someone to witness and accept them for *them*. That's who Killian was... and not just for me.

Killian respected himself and others. He would literally go to sleep in his room upstairs while we were all downstairs drinking to blackout. Unfortunately, one night when he went upstairs like his sweet self, he found me in HIS bed — and after doing a double take, my ex-high school boyfriend popped out from under the covers too. Like I said... too comfortable. Poor fucking Killian.

He was a good person; he was pure. He was also a nerd. And he saw me for who I really am, which is also a nerd. We matched intellectually and loved going to the movies. He was also the best big brother to his sister, Vivian.

Life is sad and we lose people too soon. We lose good people. Killian and I had grown distant during our college years, but losing someone that was such a safe and foundational relationship in my childhood was incredibly hard. It would be hard for anyone. However, my real grief stems from what I feel for his family. No family is ever the same after such a great tragedy, but watching them handle it with such love and strength is something I will admire forever.

I get really mad sometimes when I think about how my and Killian's relationship could have developed with age. He was a brilliant actor, singer, and performer. He didn't give a shit about what anyone thought, and that was probably my favorite thing about him. His mom also taught me one of my favorite sayings to this day, "Act like a King or Queen, and they will treat you like one." And truth be told, I still live by that today. It works.

Rest easy Kill, I love you. Justin Bieber never had shit on you man!

8

The Three Reasons: Part 1

I need to clarify again that my intention for this book is not to tell you why *you* should quit drinking. My goal is to tell you why and how *I* quit drinking. And then also why I think this choice could be beneficial to those who have a similar relationship with alcohol. Okay, *maybe* I am writing this to tell people to quit drinking. Some things just make sense, and not drinking makes sense… for a lot of people.

So, I am going to break down why I quit into three simple reasons.

1. My physical health

2. My mental & spiritual health

3. My future & purpose in life

My physical health: There are absolutely zero physical benefits to drinking alcohol. If you think there are, you're wrong and have been manipulated by consumerism (just my opinion). From my personal experience, I have only ever had negative consequences to the mind, body, and soul. A few of those include vomiting, weight gain (40 pounds at one point to be exact), inability to physically move for hours, sleep deprivation, endless regret, shame, self-hatred, and so much more.

I know that somewhere in some sort of study they say that "a glass of wine a day keeps the doctor away" or whatever, and maybe that's true, but for people like me, one glass does not exist. One glass turns into one bottle. As you know by now, I like to compare it to vampires and bloodlust. Once I start, I cannot stop until I have had enough, and enough does not exist. I usually never knew how much I would actually drink because my goal was always the same: drink until you do not feel or remember anything.

From a marketing perspective, telling people that alcohol is good for you is a great idea because I am sure they can somehow prove that one glass helps with heart functioning or whatever, and maybe it does. But I bet a glass of water with lemon helps too. Why aren't there billboards for that? Oh wait, alcohol companies are making money. A lot of money. For hundreds of years.

Since I quit drinking, I have truly never looked (or felt) better. It took about a year to see the full effects, but yes, the changes are drastic. I was drinking so much that I was sick almost every morning. I could not exercise properly. I could not work or think clearly. And I was never sleeping well. I have also lost at least twenty pounds since I quit drinking. Weight from drinking was something I struggled with for years. My depression showed in my weight. When I look back at pictures of myself, it is just so obvious. I am a naturally smaller framed girl, so it was a lot of extra weight to be carrying around for me. I looked inflamed. I looked sick. I was sick. And I felt like I was living in a body that did not belong to me.

Let me be clear, it is absolutely normal to have your weight fluctuate during life. That is OKAY and normal. But the weight I was carrying was specific. It was alcohol-fed depression weight. It was inflammation. It was exhaustion. And it was a hard cycle to get out of, but when I did, I swear my body snapped right back to how it was before I even started drinking. I am now living how I always wanted to — healthily.

How? Well, basically I went from drinking seven rum and cokes and throwing down a full vegan pizza at midnight, to sipping on kombucha after a nice homemade dinner and tucking myself into bed at 10 p.m. with frequencies on and plans to be up bright and early for my morning barre class. No more hangover food cravings. Since I quit drinking, I eat much cleaner. I don't crave any of the shit I was eating while drunk, it actually makes me sick now. My body took in so many empty calories for years that also played a role as "depression fuel." Dietary changes changed my life, and so that combined with cutting out alcohol, I have had a complete transformation. This I will swear on.

P.S. I have not always gone about being a healthy weight in the right way. I took over-the-counter weight loss pills when I was seventeen because I couldn't figure out what the hell was wrong with me. Surprise — it was binge drinking, the wrong antidepressants, and hangover eating. But back then I didn't know what I know now. I was young and uneducated. And I'm pretty sure those weight loss pills are globally banned now, so yeah... not an expert. Just a girl with a story.

Alcohol had a major effect on my habits. I have always had plenty of "good habits," exercise being a major one, but one bad habit can sabotage all the good ones, and that it did. Now, without that one bad habit (alcohol), all my good habits are stronger and helping me manifest my goals and dreams into reality. I cover more on the power of habits later, and if you have not read *Atomic Habits* by James Clear, you definitely should. Just saying.

You can reinvent yourself every single day if you want to. I am living proof. Confidence is a daily feeling for me now. Sure, I have always *seemed* like a confident girl, but I wasn't when I was drinking. It's hard to be confident when dripping with regret. However, once I started to forgive myself for my past and as I continue to work to be my best self, my confidence is back in full swing. Given, this did not happen overnight, and I still have my days of self-loathing, but my confidence comes from within now. No one can take it from me. It needs to come from your core, your spirit. It comes from treating yourself right and trusting yourself. I lost absolute trust in myself when I was drinking. You cannot be confident in something that is false and alcohol brings out false personalities. That is why it's so addictive — you get to become someone that you "aren't." However, drunk confidence is not real confidence, *sorry*.

There is also an art to arrogance. Elizabeth Gilbert wrote about this in her book *Big Magic* (another one of my favorites). She says that arrogance is our creative right. You could say that developing a "good" arrogance helped me quit, and I am even more so now because I am beating alcoholism. And that is not a bad thing. Through this arrogance, I have gained the right to love myself for all my flaws and messiness. I needed to love myself to quit, I needed to choose myself, and I needed to become cocky as fuck because how else are you going to survive in this cold hard world?

I ran cross country in high school literally because my therapist told me my body needed something intense. Cross country was brutal, but I did it because I needed to. Running helped my head. I felt like I was running off my depression every step that I took. I ran away my pain while a 50-year-old contract lawyer / coach was yelling at me to run faster, faster, and faster — up hills, big hills! He would then sit us down after every practice and give a theoretical lesson on life. I learned a lot from him. But damn that is a hard sport, and really, I just needed someone to talk to. But hey, at least I had abs!

I love myself now. You need to love yourself. And physical health is a great starting point. I could not say that I truly loved myself two years ago. I now see the girl that was drowning. The girl trying to crawl out of a dark hole. Accepting those parts of myself helped. Confidence must come from within. It is spirit based. And fortunately, when you glow within, it shows outward. I will promise you that.

Sure, quitting took work. So does physical health. You will not magically wake up one day and quit something that controls you. It takes time, patience, research, and then living and failing through that research. But again, my goal is to share my story so you can cut some of that time off. So, take my advice — prioritize your physical health and I promise you it will make your journey to alcohol sobriety, or any goal you have, much more attainable.

9

Tampons & Enemas

I always had stomach and menstrual issues growing up. They started when I first got my period at thirteen and I was *terrified* of tampons. My friend and I laid on my bed one night and she tried to put a tampon up my vagina for hours. I was screaming bloody murder every time she got just the tip of the tampon even close. I could not fathom having a finger, let alone a foreign object that was supposed to go inside of me, so close. After multiple failed attempts with multiple "helpers," no one (including myself) knew why I was so fucking scared. However, now I do — it's a little friend that I like to call *trauma*. And unfortunately, a lot of us have it. But that is not the moral of this specific story.

The moral of this story is that I had serious issues from a young age with things that were supposed to be "normal," aka periods and using the restroom. It really affected my life. One time Killian, oh poor young Killian, walked in on me and his mom in the bathroom trying to get a half-inserted tampon out of my vagina. It was stuck and I was screaming because I just could not get it out. I traumatized him, and possibly his entire family that day. Basically, what had happened was I finally had the guts to get a tampon in, but once I was halfway there, I started screaming and instead of just going through with it and pushing that sucker in, I freaked out and started trying to pull it out. But it was too dry and got stuck, so when I was pulling it out it split in half and looked like one of those everlasting ropes that magicians pull from their pockets, you know? It was bad. SO bad. And I was, of course, still screaming. Killian's mom eventually helped me get it out, but this was still just the beginning of a long journey of trying to touch my own vagina. Sure, as I am writing this I can now wear tampons (with the applicator), but at age 25, I still have yet to put my finger in my own vagina. And that makes me sad. I just want to finger bang myself already!

Okay maybe the moral of this story is that body trauma affects us in so many ways. It has made me uncomfortable in my own body for as long as I can remember and it still has me horrified to touch a part of MY own body. It also led me down a path of making choices that did not feel safe. It led me to giving my body away for much less than it deserved. There is a reason certain woman are labeled as "promiscuous," "dirty," or "overly sexual" at young ages. We had no fucking choice. We were just trying to survive.

Back to the periods, sorry boys. My bleeding was so abnormal that when I was fourteen my dad had to take me to the doctor to get on birth control. My dad was not openly communicative when it came to this kind of stuff, so this was an extremely uncomfortable road trip. I remember feeling so ashamed for needing it, but my mom was MIA and I needed to figure out what was wrong. Did I say that I was fourteen? Gosh, I was such a stressed little baby.

Then when I was around fifteen, I started having serious issues with my digestion. It started out as feeling bloated 24/7, which I dealt with for a few years. But once I turned 17, things got bad. I had very difficult bowels. It was like tar moving through my organs. I once went fourteen days without shitting. FOURTEEN. Do you know what that feels like? I felt bloated, stuck, heavy, hopeless, stressed, and pissed off. It was horrible. It also led to weight gain and many, many mental blocks. Also, more alcohol consumption. Why? Because chugging vodka would usually help me go, so there another level of dependence was born. It got so bad that when I was in high school I would wake up early in the morning before school to do an enema or put a wax suppository up my butt just to try to shit. (Unfortunately, those usually didn't work and I would sometimes have to go to school with the wax suppository still in me.) Not a good feeling, lemme tell ya. All of this only added more stress to an already stressful time. My mental health was at an all-time low. Those last two years of high school really were the worst years of my life, for many reasons, and not shitting was definitely at the top of that list. The cyber bullying and twitter account were just icing on the cake, but we will get to that part soon.

My stomach issues lasted into college. After years of trying to figure out what was wrong, I ended up cutting out dairy when I was 21. My life completely changed. My body cannot digest dairy, it just completely fucks me up. My stomach balloons up like ten times its size and I am constipated, for days. So yes, that was the problem all along. FUCKING DAIRY. Did I tell you my dad's side of the family ran a dairy farm? Wtf.

So why am I telling you all of this? Because the only cure during this time to make me feel better was alcohol. Alcohol would "help" me feel more comfortable in my body. Meanwhile, it was only making things worse. So much worse. To the average person, I did not look as bad as I felt. But I was always looking for an escape outside my body. There was just too much pain in it to bear.

Looking back, I realize how abnormal all those issues were and how extreme they got. Maybe I have always been an extremist, but the tampon and vagina issues stemmed from something darker that I had yet to put my finger on (no pun intended). And it all led me to take such poor care of myself, for so long. I didn't have the right people in my life to guide me or give me what I needed. My dad tried, but he didn't know what to do with me. His idea of what a parent is was quite different from what I actually needed. I needed extreme nurturing and affectionate love. Some people are just not able to give that.

Fortunately, I found a therapist when I was fifteen to help me survive those years. Her name was Lynn. She was my "parental figure," and without her, I don't know where I would be today.

My issues still show up today. I have full blown panic attacks every time I go to the gynecologist. In 2021, I went to a male gynecologist and during the exam I was shaking so bad that he paused, grabbed my legs, and said, "Who hurt you?" This is how tense I get when someone, whom I am not turned on by, touches down there. That is trauma in real life and it was also so beyond inappropriate for that doctor to say that to me. However, after he finished the appointment, that same doctor ended up buying 40K worth of basketball tickets from me. Made that inappropriate comment worth it, right? Well, no, that was definitely the last time I ever went to a male gynecologist. We went from legs spread open and fingers deep, to sitting in his office signing a contract. Talk about sex work! (Kidding.) Why do the strangest things always happen to me? Maybe it's because my vagina is just so damn pretty.

10

The Three Reasons: Part 2

My mental & spiritual health: Discovering my spirituality was a major contributor to my success in alcohol sobriety. Over the last few years, I have done a lot of "self-work" and "self-discovery." It all started in 2020 when one of my best friends, D'Kota, came to visit me in Atlanta and introduced me to crystals, sage, and chakra meditation. This is when my real journey began. It was as if a portal of everlasting knowledge opened up to me. Please note, by no means am I trying to push my spiritual beliefs on others, but finding a higher power to communicate with played a major role in my ability to quit drinking.

Meeting another dear friend of mine, Sheryl, played a significant impact on my journey. Sheryl is a medium and introduced me to Reiki. Reiki has helped me connect with myself and others on a deeper level. It has also helped me in the healing work with my pain body.

I don't want to get into too many details about my specific practices, but I do want everyone to know that it is possible to find something that can help. And it doesn't need to be religion or spiritual beliefs — this is just my story.

The Alchemist by Paulo Coelho also played a key role in my journey. I have given away at least twenty-five copies at this point. I really should stop buying them for all the guys I date though, it never works out after I do... usually because they never freaking read it! I just believe so deeply that everyone should experience it. Every day I feel more aligned with my personal legend and reason for being here. I needed a reason to be here. I needed a purpose. And this is just one of the few books that helped me find it.

I grew up Roman Catholic but never felt fully comfortable in that environment. There are no wrong or right answers when it comes to which God (or Goddess) you prefer to talk to, but for me, I knew I needed *something* as I have always been a spiritual person. It just took me some time to figure out what that *something* was.

This spiritual "work" is what lead me to become strong enough to quit. I have hit rock bottom countless times — for years I felt as if I was living in it. But I always knew there was a better version of myself out there. I never lost hope. I just needed help to find her, I needed spiritual guidance.

I wish we could all just come together and accept that most spiritual practices are kinda the same and that the only difference *really* is how we choose to communicate through it. Spirituality is a tool to get to know yourself and those that have come before you better. I learned a lot about myself once I started to really *listen*.

Finding my way to practice also helped me integrate with my *shadow self.* I believe we live out a lot of our mental health issues through our shadow selves. Mine thrived off my blackouts. I became her in physical form, doing shit that I would never have done without that influence. She usually ruined everything I had going for me.

Now, we talk. I understand her. I see her. I just needed to open up to a higher power to communicate properly with her. She was a hurt and damaged little girl trying to survive in this scary and challenging world. I experienced complex trauma at an early age and she helped me "hide" it from the world. But in actuality, I was not hiding anything. My darkness was clear as day when I was drinking. I was her. I still am her in many ways. I am still all of those dark nights and tragic events. But I am also all the beautiful things I have still managed to do during that time. If you are anything like me and you struggle with becoming someone "completely different" when you are drinking, and you do things that you regret, over and over, then that means you have lost control. Gaining control back over my life is the greatest thing I have ever done. No one can tell me shit I don't already know about myself. And now that, that is power.

Sure, alcohol is also a powerful *spirit*, but it's the bad kind. Ying and yang.

I have been on antidepressants since I was sixteen, which I talk about more later on. Mixing binge drinking and antidepressants is a risky ball game. It took me into an even darker shadow of myself while emerged in the depths of a blackout. Alcohol is a spirit, so mixing thus spirit with a powerful medication can lead to scary and mysterious places in the psyche. Now, I have a safer mental space and my medication is working how it always should have been.

At the end of the day, all this spiritual "work" did not pay off until I did one major thing: put down the bottle. Alcohol was the evil little spirit blocking me from the good ones that I needed to meet. And once I finally said goodbye, all the work over the years paid off. The work always counts, even if you don't see it in the moment. Mental and spiritual health are the backbone to our souls. Taking care of yourself internally will always reflect externally, and doing so helped me become strong enough to quit. That is a fucking fact.

11

Harry Harry Dicks

Okay, it's time for my least favorite story, but might as well put it out there.

The year is 2014, it is my junior year in high school, and a Twitter account was made about me called *Harry Harry Dicks.* It was a Twitter account specifically curated with edited images taken from my Facebook. Images that just so happened to have multiple drawn on dicks going straight into my mouth and/or vaginal area, paired with gags and a "funny" play of words. Basically what we would call memes today. For example, one image was a photoshopped picture of me with a drawn-on dick going straight into my mouth and words saying, "I'm not saying she is a slut but... her favorite shade of lip gloss is penis." Another one is a picture of me smiling with my thumbs up and the words, "I'M A GIANT WHORE." Then another is a picture of me bent over, please remember I was sixteen at the time, that says, "I want love but I'm too busy sucking dick, xoxo." And then another that has my face cropped on a box of Oreos titled, "WHOREO." I'll give it to them, that one was creative. But still, not fun to see. And I unfortunately still have all the screenshots today to prove it. This was also at a time when Twitter was extremely popular at my school. Icing on top.

The account was created a few weeks after I had a bad blackout and slept with one of my male "friends" who had been dating a girl that had recently survived cancer. I mention her having cancer because she did, and she had just gotten over it, so it was pretty fucked up of me to sleep with her "boyfriend." (They were on a break!) She was our high schools "surviving sweetheart." But let me be clear, this girl was never a sweetheart — she was a bitch. *Excuse my French.* I don't hold any resentment now because we were kids and people change, but back then she was basically the Regina George of our high school... with cancer. I didn't stand a chance.

The funny thing though is that I don't even remember it happening. The night it happened was my first time not remembering having sex, and he was also only the second person I had ever slept with, the first being my ex-boyfriend. This situation fucked me up and started my journey with sex as self-abuse. Yes, sex can be a form of self-abuse.

This guy and I ending up sleeping together again a few days later, so that time I do remember, and yes, I know that's fucked up. I think we were both just so traumatized by how the girl was treating us and we needed to bond. We also were such great friends for years and definitely had some puppy love for each other, but still, we were dumb for that and were both seriously terrified of Regina. And yes, let's call her Regina now. Once Regina found out, the guy called me and said that we need to lie and say nothing happened, so I texted her saying that exact thing. LIES. Bad Elli!

I felt bad for lying, and of course just how *karma* always works, the boy ended up admitting everything to her. When he told her the truth, it made me look like the villain and a liar. Which technically I was at the time, not my proudest moment, but still, it didn't feel fair.

It is very hard for me to write this out now. My drinking patterns worsened after this whole fiasco and I was only sixteen years old when it happened. I fucked up, and it was at the hand of alcohol. I had to face consequences that my little brain was not ready to handle. I was always the bad person. Bad because my drinking made me do shit that I would never have done without it. I had at least twenty *bad* blackouts before the age of 16, this being the first involving sex, and I still had a long road ahead of me of the same behavior, if not worse. You do the math. Bad shit happened. A lot of bad shit.

But okay, after that night occurred and Regina found out what happened, she started to follow me around to my classes and yell at me calling me a whore or whatever. She would also tweet horrible things about me. One of the tweets was about my eyebrows being too fluffy and them needing to be waxed, so after that I started getting them done, and they do look a lot better now. So, hey, at least I got some advice out of it. Teenage girls can be such assholes. I was in such a state of disassociation walking around school for months. I think I always knew I was above treating people like how she treated me, so I acted like I didn't even care after a while, but I absolutely did. What sucked too was that we had a lot of mutual friends, which meant I started to be uninvited to parties, which meant fewer drinking events. Sad day for an alcoholic. The people, including my "friends," around me knew that the way she was treating me was uncalled for, but no one stood up for me. No. Fucking. One. That part really sucked and I honestly do think the cancer card had something to do with it. I was the *villain,* at least to everyone else, so I started to believe it too. *A dumb desperate whore.* I stayed unresponsive to her threats, deleted my social media, and kept my head down until the weekend when I could drink again. Except then, I had to get creative with my drinking. This period was the first time I drank alone. I had a handle of Vladimir Vodka in my closet and would drink it after school. Pretty fucking sad for a sixteen-year-old girl.

Back to the Twitter account. It was created about a week after the bad blackout. The night that I first saw that account I remember going down to my basement and falling against the wall, fully hyperventilating. My mom was living in Virginia, my best friend had just left back to Milwaukee, and my dad and stepmom were not easy to talk to about these sorts of things. I was *alone,* living in a house with people that didn't know how to give the love and support I needed. When I found the account, so did the entire high school. My ex-boyfriend, who had broken my heart that same year, reached out to me first. He told me he was sorry and that it was fucked up. For some reason hearing from him made me feel better, it gave me hope. Sad little Elli.

That same night I finally got the guts to tell my dad what was going on. He is not very emotionally capable when it comes to these kinds of things, so his first idea was to call the police, and that he did. He ended up sending the police to Regina's house and it turns out the guy I slept with was in her basement and they were eating pizza or some shit. The police officer called my dad and said verbatim, "*Regina* says she did not make the account, but she was crying and screaming that 'Elli fucked my boyfriend!'" And that my friends, is how my dad found out that I was not a virgin.

I received very little sympathy from my father after the police officer said those words. I remember being upstairs in my bathroom and his eyes went dark. It is something I will never forget. I was alone after that moment. Just me and *Harry Harry Dicks*. No father wants to hear his daughter lost her "virginity" from a local police officer, but still, I could have *really* used a hug from someone that loved me, not more shame.

The even sadder part about all of this is that about a month later I discovered that the masterminds behind *Harry Harry Dicks* were most likely a group of girls who I considered to be my "friends." I have no proof or admittance from them to this day, but they know who they are. The point here is to not have a confession, but to make people like them realize that these types of things can change the course of someone's life forever. My life was changed *forever* after this account. I still have PTSD trying to use Twitter. Sometimes I wish I just knew why they created it. Most people will say it was jealousy, but I couldn't understand *why* because I fucking hated myself back then. Maybe creating this account was a way for them to seem cool to Regina and have some sort of "power" over me. But why would that power even be necessary? I guess it's a good thing I can't comprehend the bully mindset. Also, it *really* pissed me off to think about the guy in this situation. He had his girlfriend and all of his friends back within a week. He was living the dream. Me? Not so much.

This whole situation broke me very deeply, but I took the "high road" as my father likes to call it. I never responded to anything, kept my head down, and worked hard in school. I realize now how traumatized I was at the time. Suppressing what I was going through and taking the "high road" only led me to drowning in other ways. Self-hate, suppression, anger, and *a bottle of vodka* is not a good combination. It all only made my drinking worse. Those last two years of high school were rough and consisted of a lot of depressive drinking. I started giving my body away more easily and more often after this account was made. My number of sexual partners went from two to *too many* during the remaining years of high school, remembering barely any of the newer partners. Those basements got darker and scarier, quickly.

Leaving Pennsylvania to go to school in Colorado was the best decision I could have made. I needed a fresh slate, away from *Harry Harry Dicks* and mean little bitches.

A few years later, Regina apologized to me at a concert in Pittsburgh for everything. I appreciated that and I don't consider her to be a bad person, but one of my biggest realizations today is that she probably had love and support after that night with the police officer, while I was stuck with aggressive cyber bullying and a father that now looked at me like I was a whore. There is a reason my skin is so tough. I had no *choice*. I learned young, and a little too aggressively, that people can be cruel and life is not always fair.

I also wish I knew back then that everything was not my fault. Every time I felt so low that I couldn't find a way to get back up, I would search for another party and drink, in hopes that things would be different. For years I thought the only way to feel better about my mistakes was to get drunk and make better memories. But that never happened, not until I quit.

Maybe there are a few positives from it all too. Now I can use those girls and this whole situation as a trigger for my acting when I need to channel being really hurt. It works pretty damn well. Also, in a way, it is flattering that those girls took so much time out of their lives to make those photo memes of me. Photoshop was not easy to use back in 2014, and I will say that the name *Harry Harry Dicks* was creative. It makes for a really great book chapter, lol.

I just wanted to be liked and when you give that power to others it makes that *want* impossible.

Getting bullied was common in my family. My mom and both of my brothers were bullied in high school. My mom actually had a large wooden dick shoved in her locker with Elmer's glue all over it around the same age as me in this story. Generational trauma much? I believe that bullies attack the kinder people in this world. They are jealous of good hearts and want to make others feel as wretched as they do, and that is sad. I am grateful I was able to get through it, and I want others to know that they can too.

High school girls are mean and forgiveness is important. Am I still angry with these girls? No. I wish them the best. Just from a very very very far and distant place, but still, the best! I was hesitant to put this specific story in here, but this event is what took my need for drinking to the next level, and soon after, I was put on antidepressants for the first time because my mental health had plummeted so low. My years of abuse were just beginning and I hid how terrible things were to those closest to me. I channeled it all into my shadow.

I hope letting others read this story will give me the peace I have always craved. I never told anyone in college or my adult years about it. I have kept it hidden, like some dark shameful secret. Those days end here.

P.S. I was never a whore, whores get paid. I was a slut. ☺ (At least this is what my mom told me.)

12

The Three Reasons: Part 3

My future & purpose in life: Alcohol would have ruined my future, that's a fact. It was so clear, but for a long time I just didn't even care. Okay, I cared, but not enough to quit. That was until I discovered something incredibly special to me while alone in that Midtown Atlanta apartment, something that became my most powerful "last straw."

Acting played a significant role in how I was initially able to quit drinking. It was not until I felt like I found a true purpose in life that I needed to quit. I had a choice to make — either I quit and pursued my dreams, or I kept drinking and put them to the side. Let me be clear, your purpose does not have to be a career change or a massive shift in life. Again, this is just my story and what led *me* to alcohol sobriety. I am simply providing a blueprint model that can be replicated and edited. And finally pursuing my dreams and living in my "purpose" is what helped drop that underlying feeling or need that alcohol had filled for so long.

My acting career would have lasted two days if I were still drinking. Maybe I am exaggerating, I tend to do that sometimes, but I really do believe it. Alcohol was the last thing holding me back from following my dreams because it is the one thing that could have destroyed them all. I was addicted to binge drinking and escaping. That is not a good look in the entertainment industry, or any industry really. Addiction is a controller. I was controlled. And sometimes that control led me to do questionable things. Addiction does not care who you are or what you do. If it has control over you, it will always win.

I am confident that I am destined to do great things, not in a cocky way, but in a way where I could either accept that and move accordingly, or I could have kept partying and suppressing everything in my gut telling me what I needed to do. That is where most of our depression stems from, suppressing what you truly want and what you need to do to get there, because it's hard.

Acting was my purpose strike, yours probably won't be that, but if it is then fuck ya, go for it. A straightforward way to figure out your higher purpose or "what you should be doing" is to ask yourself, "What am I good at?" When things come naturally to us, it probably means we are supposed to be doing them. I am not a singer, because I cannot sing. But if I could, I promise you I would be singing from the rooftop every day because that would be what I am "supposed" to do. The same is with any kind of gift. If you are good at something, that is a gift. Use it. Nurture it. If you say you are not good at anything, then I don't know what to tell you because you are lying. And if your response is that you are good at drinking, then congrats and good luck. I really mean it.

I am special, but I am not *special*. I say this a lot. What I mean is that I am special, but so is everyone else. We are all special and have the right to feel so. And since I somewhat know myself now, I know that to carry out something great, I need 100% of my energy. I want to be a superhuman. I want to make massive changes in this world. And so, alcohol needed to be removed. Acting was the final big straw in my head on May 4th, 2022. I found something I really loved to do, something that I felt a calling towards, and something that I am honestly pretty good at. How could I not go all in? I want to get to the levels that I see myself at when it comes to writing, acting, and creating, which means I cannot be incapable of getting up in the morning. I need to be at 100%. I want to be at 100%. I like working. I like creating. I do not like having my head over a toilet throwing up stomach acid every other day. It set me back. I was sick, always fucking sick. You can't get shit done when you're sick.

I am ready to be in rooms with people who have accomplished what I dream about. I am ready for higher conversations. I am ready to be invited, and not just as a plus one. In order for me to do these things, I need to be sober from alcohol. It took a lot to get to the point of being ready to put something else, aka myself, before it. For so long my identity was alcohol. I was a partier and I loved to throw parties. It was what I did. I no longer do that. Hence why I am ready for the next phase of my life. My identity is no longer an "alcoholic party girl." I am more than that. I always was. It just took me some time to see it. I needed to remove the blurry lens I had on for so long. I thought I could never give it up, but I did. So can you.

Also, I have always been the kind of person that if I say I am going to do something, I do it. I get it done. For example, every time I said I was going to blackout, I did. Haha. Okay on a more uplifting note... I said I was going to become an actor, and I did. I said I was going to become a writer, now I am one. I said I was going to be sober from alcohol, now I am. All my hard work and efforts over the years paid off, even though it never felt like they would. I decided to believe in myself. I guess that is also one of my gifts — belief. We are entitled to our gifts. Arrogance is not a bad thing. Arrogance brought me back to my power. I am entitled to live the way that I want to live. So are you.

Now, I am not afraid to say the shit that I feel. I'll say it now with my motha fuckin' chest! Why? Because I know that speaking up for myself is going to help me on the path I am heading. Please keep in mind, I would not be this way without years of being silenced. It took me time to get here, but I am here now, and I am not going anywhere... unless I decide to. Then I will go wherever I want to. You, see? We ARE in control. Stop believing all the bullshit that you are not, you are. No one else is inside your head, just you. Make it a good place to be.

I am not perfect, never have been, never will be. I can have bad days. I can be an egotistical bitch. I can be brutally honest and unfiltered. I can be annoying and needy. I can be rude for no apparent reason. I can be weak. But the key is, I no longer *am* these things. That is the mental shift I had after I quit drinking. We do not have to put ourselves in these boxes of who or what we think we "are." Shit changes. People change. Change is inevitable and it's also fucking beautiful if you let it happen. Let change wash over you. I did, and it "changed" my life. Obviously.

Emotions are powerful. I am a very emotional person. Something that I tried to hide for so long. But now, I have chosen a career that embodies emotions. You see? That is purpose. Now is NOT the time to suppress our emotions. There is *beauty* in vulnerability. We are all beings of light and love. We are each made up of energy, we are all various different swirls of that energy, and love is what holds us together. Human intelligence and physical form all stem from energy. So, if we are all just energy, why would we not be able to make massive shifts and changes? Energy moves. We are not meant to stay stagnant and conform to these rules and regulations that were designed for us. What they want is for us to work, eat, drink, sleep, repeat. Work for what? This company that doesn't give a shit about me?! They want us to be robots confined to these straight lines that lead us right off a fucking cliff. Those days are over, at least for me. My purpose is bigger than that. Most of ours are. I want to help others step into their own personal power. And so, I will do that by living and growing into my own and then writing about it. I think this will work. At least for now.

We all have treasures hidden within us. Sometimes you just have to go deep to find them — and with depth, usually comes darkness. An example of my own darkness is that sometimes I get scared that I started acting too late and that time is going by too fast and that mine will eventually run out. But this is not true, you see, because you can never be too old to be an actress. These are just restrictions I have created in my mind based on *fear*. I am not invincible and I am still scared and stressed as shit at times, but the difference now is that I will never give up. We must always fight the good fight.

13

X's Basement

During my senior year of high school, I was part of a friend group where all we did was drink and party on the weekends. Not regular partying, think more like getting absolutely demolished. That was the mission, at least for me. Those nights in question contributed to why my senior year of high school was one of the worst years of my life. During this year my mom was living in Downtown Pittsburgh serving time on house arrest with no driver's license. And my dad and stepmom spent almost every weekend at their lake house, so I was alone... a lot. That loneliness led me to constantly seek people to be around, and of course, I chose people that shared the same coping mechanisms as I did — binge drinking

My friend, let us call him X, had parents who let him use their basement as his own area to live in, and really just do whatever he wanted. Most nights that I was there were spent binge drinking. And most of those nights were bad. Back during my junior year, I blacked out so hard in his basement that I projectile vomited all over his bathroom and he had to clean it up. I don't remember a thing. That incident was right after my first boyfriend broke up with me, a time when I really was not okay. X was so mad at me. He is allergic to alcohol so he barely drank, he just smoked a lot. Which meant he remembered everything. If you are reading this X, thank you for that.

I got along most with people in high school who partied because we all lacked parental supervision, and a lot of us still have addiction issues today. Pittsburgh is a tough place for kids with this kind of up bringing, take it from a pro. But okay, back to that night my senior year.

I remember drinking a lot this specific night and the boy who was involved in the Twitter fiasco also being there, considering he is X's best friend. The night was a complete blur, and when I woke up on X's couch the next morning I had this horrible throbbing pain in my hand. When I looked down, I screamed. My thumb was so fucked up, most definitely broken. I do not remember how or during what part of the night it happened, and that was very scary. I asked the guys who were still there if they knew what happened and they said no. Classic. However, in that moment, I had three flashbacks. And they were also very scary.

First, I had a vivid memory of running through snow and falling. Second, one of me verbally fighting in the back room with the *Twitter guy*. And third, one that really scared me. Also one that I did not accept as real until after I quit drinking. In this third memory, I was walking around the upstairs of X's house butt ass naked and walked into X's parent's bedroom when they were asleep. I was standing at the entrance of their bedroom door like a fucking walking demon. What really concerned me about this memory is that by that point, I had never been upstairs, but I have an exact memory of what everything looked like. I have actually never told anyone this story, including X, and I am still not sure if his parents ever saw me. But part of me thinks they did, and they just never said anything. A few years later, I was back at X's and I went upstairs for the "first time" sober-ish, and to my astonishment, the upstairs layout was exactly as I saw it in my blackout memory. This moment still haunts me to this day. Also, X, if you are reading this, I am so sorry. That was really fucked up.

I like to pretend that night never happened and part of me really hopes the part where I was naked in front of his parent's room was just a dream, but I don't think it was. I lied to my dad the next day about how I broke my hand and said I fell running in the snow, resulting in me getting my first cast. I got hurt a lot when I was drinking. Massive bruises on my legs and arms were weekly remembrances of blacked out weekends. But breaking my thumb that night really scared me. I was so fucked mentally and now physically too. How I broke my hand will be something I'll wonder about for the rest of my life, but at least I didn't feel it. Haha. Okay, I actually can't write about this night anymore, the part with the guy from the Twitter fiasco was even worse. He always made me cry because for some reason... I *loved* him.

There were reasons I was drinking to blackout every weekend. I was drowning in pain with no one to talk to. My previous boyfriend's mom was always so concerned about me and why I constantly needed rides, and then when she would drop me off... no one was ever home. I was alone too much. My dad didn't want everyone to know our "business" so I never told anyone why, but then that just left me stuck. I was fucking stuck trying to self soothe in a poison that wanted me dead, with no one around that seemed to care.

Oh, poor young Elli with so much to still learn about life.

Don't Put Me in A Box: Does anyone truly know you? I mean think about it. Every day you wake up and you are alone with your thoughts. You might think a million thoughts a day, but who can really know any of what you are actually thinking? I am not sure if anyone has ever fully known someone inside and out. Hell, I am still learning to know my damn self. I am by no way lessening connections and relationships with deep ties and years of loving someone. But isn't it interesting to think about how many thoughts we have a day and only ever verbalize around 1% of them?

So then why do we let others judge us? Why do we let other people's opinions affect our decision making? Why do I need someone else's opinion who can only TRY to understand 1% of all my thoughts and feelings? Sure, this 1% is different for everyone. Perhaps you are someone who feels like they say everything they are thinking. But are you really? If you are thinking about saying more than 1% of what you are thinking, then, in reality, you are thinking on a deeper level than the so called "everything" that you express. Is that not half the thought itself?

So ya, don't put me in a fucking box.

14

Alcohol Use Disorder

What is alcohol use disorder?

Well, let's first start off with that the term "alcoholic" can come off… unflattering. I prefer to use the term "alcohol use disorder" (AUD) when describing my toxic relationship with alcohol. Or sometimes "binge drinking disorder," I like that one too. That is also what every single one of my therapists have diagnosed me with, which I'm not even sure they are allowed to do. Again, this is all just information from my non-doctor, non-scientist noggin.

What I do know is that I have a fucking problem with alcohol and saying, "Hi, I'm Elli and I struggle with alcohol use disorder," feels less dramatic than saying, "Hi, I'm Elli and I'm an alcoholic."

The National Institute on Alcohol Abuse and Alcoholism (NIAAA, 2023) defines alcohol use disorder as, "a medical condition characterized by an impaired ability to stop or control alcohol use despite adverse social, occupational, or health consequences."

Sounds about right. Also, please remember that alcohol does not affect everyone the same way it affects me. I have an addictive personality. Once I start, I cannot stop. *Vampire.*

I like to think that AUD is becoming the modern and more commonly used term for alcoholism. AUD doesn't put anyone in a box. There are levels to it. Think of it like a spectrum. You can have anywhere from a very low to a very high-level of it. Unlike alcoholism, where you are just an "alcoholic" and nothing else. That doesn't work for us anymore, especially with how common alcohol abuse is these days.

Addiction is genetic, but also a bit random. Not everyone in my family has AUD, but a good amount of us do. Luck of the draw you could say. So, it is safe to say that not everyone in a family line will struggle with the same issues, but some will. That's why it is so important to understand what something like AUD, or whatever challenge it may be, looks like so we can better support the ones we love.

For example, instead of getting mad at your loved one for getting "too drunk" every single time you go out, maybe you can look at them with a difference lens and say, "Oh shit, you might not be able to control it! Let me help you dig deeper into this rather than make you feel even more guilty for your decisions and what you cannot necessarily control. Let me support you in not drinking, because I love you."

This approach would help a lot of relationships in the most simplistic way possible. It is very important to try and understand drinkers and why they "can't just stop." Some people have it, some people don't. It really is as simple as that.

Below are common self-diagnosed symptoms of AUD that I found while doing my research. Alcohol addiction is a *disease*. A disease I fed for years because I was told it is good, fun, and "what you do." I was told these things on television, billboards, and in every damn magazine. We live in a world with twisted marketing tactics surrounding alcohol, something I will talk about more later. Please know it is not my intention to attack; it is my intention to speak my truth, something we are all entitled to.

Mayo Clinic wrote, "Alcohol use disorder can be mild, moderate, or severe, based on the number of symptoms you experience. Signs and symptoms may include:

1. Being unable to limit the amount of alcohol you drink.

2. Wanting to cut down on how much you drink or making unsuccessful attempts to do so.

3. Spending a lot of time drinking, getting alcohol, or recovering from alcohol use.

4. Feeling a strong craving or urge to drink alcohol.

5. Failing to fulfill major obligations at work, school, or home due to repeated alcohol use.

6. Continuing to drink alcohol even though you know it's causing physical, social, work, or relationship problems.

7. Giving up or reducing social and work activities to use alcohol.

8. Using alcohol in situations where it's not safe, such as when driving or swimming.

9. Developing a tolerance to alcohol so you need more to feel its effect, or you have a reduced effect from the same amount.

10. Experiencing withdrawal symptoms — such as nausea, sweating, and shaking — when you don't drink, or drinking to avoid these symptoms." (Mayo Clinic, 2022)

I don't know about you, but I know a lot of people that struggle with these things, which means it's a problem. A universal problem. Now, I will give you an example of each of these symptoms during my own exploration. I hope this helps.

Elli's Personal Examples:

1. *Being unable to limit the amount of alcohol you drink:* Every single

fucking time. Yes.

2. *Wanting to cut down on how much you drink or making unsuccessful attempts to do so:* I wanted to quit after every blackout. I have tried to go "30 days sober" prior to finally quitting countless times. I never made it past 10 days, usually couldn't even go 48-72 hours. So, yes.

3. *Spending a lot of time drinking, getting alcohol, or recovering from alcohol use:* This got worse once I turned 21 and could get the alcohol myself. But either way, I was always bringing alcohol to events or having parties and hangouts — fully stocked. A high percentage of my days during those 10 years involved thinking, planning, preparing, and then recovering from drinking and partying. Yes.

4. *Feeling a strong craving or urge to drink alcohol:* Every day. I needed to quiet the voices in my head, but all they ever told me was to drink. I was so controlled, for so long. Yes.

5. *Failing to fulfill major obligations at work, school, or home due to repeated alcohol use:* I would say that 99% of my "sick days" or "sorry I can't, I'm sick" moments were alcohol induced. I have missed out on a lot of great opportunities because of alcohol poising or hangovers. I was so used to throwing up stomach acid that it was not even a big deal for me after a few years. It's so gross to look back on. However, I never had to get my stomach pumped, and I like to look at that as a win. I was always scared it would happen one day though. Yes, again.

6. *Continuing to drink alcohol even though you know it's causing physical, social, work, or relationship problems:* Majority of all my problems stemmed from alcohol abuse. I have always had other problems too, but those problems never really gave me the same level of pain like alcohol did. Alcohol caused me daily anxiety and clouded judgment. Alcohol would have me headfirst in the toilet for 18+ hours. Alcohol had me sleeping through my alarm because I was blackout drunk

and left my phone in the hallway. My "problems" now feel good in comparison. It feels like I have "normal" problems now. So yes, duh.

7. *Giving up or reducing social and work activities to use alcohol:* Yes and no for this one. I would use social gatherings and events as a way to give myself a reason to drink. I was a "social butterfly" and "party girl." But the truth is that I am actually a homebody and occasional social butterfly. I am an introverted extrovert. I am a Taurus. I need to be grounded and alone. I never wanted to be a "party girl," it is what I needed to be so my drinking problem didn't look like a *drinking problem*. I worked hard to cover up my illness. AUD is an illness with symptoms that look like bad behavior. Covid-19 changed my drinking style. I was drinking 1-2 bottles of wine a night by myself, so being home didn't change the levels I was drinking after some time. I also don't think my drinking ever got worse or better throughout the 10 years because it was always extreme. I would just have to wait for the next bad event to happen that would send me into a 3-day deep depression. I talk more about the "72-hour rule" later on. I was just always trying to get away with being able to drink successfully, but that is a losing battle. So, yes.

8. *Using alcohol in situations where it's not safe, such as when driving or swimming:* I never was a drunk driver. I can count on my hand how many times I have done it, but during my last two years drinking, that is when most of the fingers would start to stand up. I scared myself once in 2021, and I was lucky nothing happened. There is no happy ending to drinking and driving. Just don't do it. And swimming? Yes, lol. Yes, yes, yes.

9. *Developing a tolerance to alcohol so you need more to feel its effect, or you have a reduced effect from the same amount:* I never learned my limit. I would just aim for turning off the lights in my head, and all of the drinking after that was just a waste. I don't even know how much

alcohol I consumed most of the time. I would just drink until it was all gone, or until I was gone. Yes.

10. *Experiencing withdrawal symptoms — such as nausea, sweating, and shaking — when you don't drink, or drinking to avoid these symptoms:* They say the best way to cure a hangover is to drink more, right? I would day drink a lot, let's just leave this there. It all became such a psychological game for me. I was in deep. So, yes.

10/10. 100%. A+. On the...
Alcohol Use Disorder Entrance Exam.

Clearly, I have this shit. And I know I am not the only one who does. If you can relate to any of these symptoms, even on a minor level, I highly recommend that you do your own *research*.

Okay, time for some *fun facts*. I saw a video online (can't remember where) that talked about how we crave alcohol because it slows down our thoughts and numbs our emotions. Alcohol is a nervous system depressant, so sure, it is easy to want to drink when we feel overstimulated, thinking that it will "chill you out." But really, this powerful **toxin** does the opposite long term. Short term solutions usually do result in long term pain.

Some more "scientificy" (again, not a scientist nor doctor) information on alcohol is that it actually dampens activity in the extended amygdala (I had to do some more Googling about this one, not good), it reduces activity in the Central Nervous System (CNS), it reduces fight or flight response, and it decreases dopamine. So basically... debilitating poison?

Also, alcohol activates the part of our brain associated with attachment. So, this is probably why you are so obsessed with that gross guy from the bar last weekend that you made out with, who also never called you back. Listen, your brain is confused. He is NOT the one. Gosh, alcohol will have you looking so fucking stupid.

I digress...

2025 Note: Throughout this book I use the term AUD more frequently than alcoholism or alcoholic. However, now being over three years alcohol-free, I am comfortable calling myself an alcoholic and referring to my illness as alcoholism. I was hyper-sensitive these first two years and using the more scientific term (AUD) made me feel better. Sure, it is still technically the "correct" term, but I am not going around telling people I have alcohol use disorder, lol. I'm a fucking *alcoholic*.

It's okay to give ourselves grace. Baby steps y'all, *baby steps.*

15

My Mom Is an "Alcoholic" & My Dad Wears a MAGA Hat

My parents are two very intelligent individuals, which is probably why they were able to escape their small middle of bumfuck nowhere Pennsylvania towns. They met at the University of Pittsburgh in the 80's, and after they graduated, they got married and had three incredible kids: Elli (the most incredible), M, and A. I am the baby, M is two years older, and A is four years older.

My parents divorced when I was four. My mom never remarried, but she sure was engaged a few times. My dad married my stepmom when I was seven, and then she and her son C, whom I consider my third brother, moved in — ta-da — our mixed family was born. M, A, and I went back and forth every other week between our moms and dads for the majority of our childhood. Well, until my mom lost her job and had to sell her house when I was in the eighth grade. That is when everything started to change.

I am sure that both of my parents have their own suitcases full of childhood trauma. That's the thing — *everyone has it.* Looking back now, I am able to appreciate my parents for who they are, what they went through, and what they gave me. No matter how badly I wanted to run away as a little girl, I wouldn't want my parents to be anyone else. And fortunately, my relationships with these two have only gotten better with age. But still, I have to talk about how they fucked me up first.

My Mom Is An "Alcoholic"

My mom was officially labeled as an "alcoholic" when I was 14 years old. This is when I was first imprinted with the idea that because she was identified as that, then she was therefore "bad."

It really affected the way I looked at her, and how family and friends treated her. I would get so mad at her when she drank. I honestly wanted to kill her at times. I would scream bloody murder at her right in her face when she was blacked out, knowing damn well she could not hear me. Funny thing is, I was usually drunk myself when yelling at her, or hungover. Like mother like daughter, am I right? I don't know if I have ever screamed at anyone as loud as I have to her. I think I was screaming at myself too, just so mad at this shitty ass habit and addiction we both seemed to share.

My mom got herself into a good amount of trouble when I was growing up, which is why she was labeled so strictly. I guess two DUI's over ten years meant you were an "alcoholic," no ifs, ands, or buts about it. I mean sure, she absolutely had a problem with drinking, most people in my family do, but labeling her so strictly as an "alcoholic" only made things *harder* for her. Because now, if she messed up and had one drink, she was already a "bad" person for it, so why not go balls to the walls and have ten? I understand this woman more now, but little 14-year-old Elli was not prepared for what was ahead of her.

Things got especially challenging for my mom when she lost her job in 2008, which was then followed by a bad engagement with another not-shit man. My mom was a mechanical engineer making over six figures and all of that was taken away overnight. And she was alone. It was a combination of these things and AUD that got her multiple DUI's, a night in jail on her 50th birthday, house arrest, and an ankle bracelet at my high school graduation. Yes, my mother wore an ankle bracelet to my high school graduation. Not the cute kind, the kind that would go off if she left her apartment outside of court approved hours. And yes, we will be calling her mother now.

My mother's circumstances made her addiction worse. Everyone closest to her judging her and blaming her only made her situation harder, which therefore led her to drink even more. My great grandmother permitted her drinking beers in the kitchen by the time she was twelve years old, and I would be lying if I didn't say my mother is the one who taught me to drink too. But she was doing her best. We all were.

But still, I watched alcohol take away my best friend during prominent years of my childhood, years when I needed her the most. I watched my mother go through some dark shit, all while trying to navigate my own at such a young age. I have seen my mother almost dead... a few times. Drunk suicidal nights are a scary thing for a 14-year-old girl, even more so when they are your mother's, not your own. I'll say this once: it is not easy to hear your mother say that she wants to die, but it sure does change your understanding on the hierarchy of life. That hierarchy being: *life and death.*

No matter what happened, all the screaming fights and traumatizing visuals, everything that we went through, got *me* to the point of being able to quit. I don't know if I would have quit this young, or ever, without watching what alcohol did to my mother. Maybe I would be living out her narrative and my daughter would be living mine, something that I wouldn't want for her. So, it is best that it was me. Also, since I quit, I have not personally seen my mother take a sip of alcohol. That is a win in my book.

My mother is magic, she always has been. Beautiful inside and out. And she is a victim of a society that makes it impossible for people that are "different" to survive. I was watching firsthand the darkest period of a powerful women's life. A period that this woman probably would not have been able to survive without her super cute little mini alcoholic daughter named Elli. We survived that period together.

I do not resent my mother for her choices; she was doing her best. But I do know that if she had more information and tools back then to identify and communicate her relationship with alcohol, things would have been easier for her. She would have had to bear less weight and could have properly explained her addiction without immediate judgment and dismissing. I dismissed her, we all did. Once she took a sip, she was a criminal in my eyes. This was before I knew what I do now.

It is safe to say that I would be writing differently about my mother if this were three years ago. This is what we call growth. The relationship dynamic between my mother and me has been filled with love, anger, excitement, worry, horror, sometimes hate, and most importantly — beauty. Our relationship has been high, low, warped, destroyed, killed, and eventually reborn. My mother is one of my soulmates. The level that we can relate and understand each other is natural and familiar. I tried to fight so long to not be like her, but the truth is, I am just like her. And what I have come to realize is that I find her to be the most beautiful and magical woman alive. Everything that we've gone through has gotten us to a point of unconditional love, and most importantly, mutual respect.

Cancer (ugh)

My mom (yes, mom again) was diagnosed with Non-Hodgkin's Lymphoma in April of 2023. This news triggered a whole new level of my awakening. It's funny, it was almost the exact day of my one-year *sober* mark.

I was in an acting class in July of 2023, and we were sharing different triggers we use to go to a dark place for a scene or character. The first thing that came to mind to share as an "emotional cry trigger" was my mom getting diagnosed with cancer earlier that year. I thought that would be an easy one because cancer always makes people cry, right? Well, no, because when I dove deeper, I had to ask myself, "How the hell do you process and bring out a 'sad' emotion when really, it triggers a somewhat opposite emotion, all at the same time?"

Let me explain — the second I thought about my mom getting diagnosed, I was immediately filled with devastation, but that devastation quickly turned into me thinking about how fucking grateful I am that I quit drinking because I do not know how I would have been able to get through that shit if I didn't.

And then I am filled with... relief, because I think about how AUD is something both my mom and I share, and to think about all of the pain and discomfort and trauma it caused, and how that pain was uncontrollable, but cancer wasn't. We could get through cancer. It was going to a be a walk in the park compared to *alcoholism*. Right? (My mom's cancer was diagnosed as highly treatable.) So yeah, confusing.

My decision to quit has affected everyone that I am close with, mostly those who also struggle with addiction themselves, *especially* my mother. Those who knew me when I was drinking will all tell you the same thing — I've changed, on massive levels. And I would not be where I am today without my mom and watching her fight the same battle. And for that, I am forever grateful.

My mom underwent seven months of intense chemotherapy and was officially cancer free in November 2023. We spent that last month of the year together down in Sarasota, Florida. No alcohol in sight. We healed. We are constantly healing each other.

Some background on my mom is that she was a Steelers groupie in her thirties — a thriving divorcé. I had so many "stepdads" that we would watch on TV every Sunday. She also rocked some of the cutest dresses and skirts when she had her ankle bracelet, never trying to hide it. It was so obvious. What a queen. She is my heart.

One of my favorite quotes is something my mom taught me that she learned from my great-grandmother. That is, "Everything that you give with no restrictions, you will get back two-fold. So, keep giving." We are givers in this family, and I wouldn't want it any other way.

Okay... I tell these next stories because I have learned in adulthood that I have an underlining fear of things, and people, disappearing or being taken away from me. Certain events happened in my childhood, these few being minor examples, that created a massive fear that I am just now recognizing and having to deal with. So much that I loved was taken away from me and there was nothing I could do about it. And it hurt. So badly. Badly enough to make me want to try and control it from ever happening again, therefore creating *control issues*. Being alcohol-free has made me have to face these patterns headfirst and I am still far from healing them. But it's the effort that counts, right?

Trauma experienced during childhood leaks into adulthood — for everyone. And for me, it is trauma that I didn't even know existed until I was on the other side of addiction. And unfortunately, a lot of these traumas can only be healed by being triggered and having to work through them soberly. And my god it fucking sucks.

I almost had a sister

When I was thirteen my mom was engaged to a pro-golfer. At this time, she was living in a nice townhome and we were still going back and forth every week between her and my dad's. I loved that townhome. When she and the pro-golfer got engaged, we ended up having to move into a bigger house for *all* of us to live in. That being my mom, the pro-golfer, my two brothers, and my new sister, *A*.

I don't remember everything from this period of time, but I do remember that I loved having a big sister. One day we went to the mall and got matching outfits and took an entire photo shoot in my room. I then took every photograph from the day and turned them into a scrapbook for her. She was a freshman in high school, so to me — she was the coolest person to ever exist.

After we moved into the bigger house, things slowly took a turn for my mom and the pro-golfer. He ended up being very... *eh*. One week, not long after we moved into this bigger and more expensive house, I went back over to my mom's and my "sister" was gone. They both were gone. Poof. No more sister for little Elli. This was not the first time this sort of thing happened. And that was the last time I ever saw *A*.

To be honest, I forgot about *A* until 2021. It wasn't until I was scrolling on Facebook and saw a familiar face that I just couldn't quite put my finger on. I was like, *I know this girl!* I know her well. Who is this?! And then, bam — memory came back. I immediately started to cry.

The even shittier part is that if we didn't move into that more expensive house, my mom might have been in a totally different situation when she lost her job a few years later. No wonder I hate golf.

Wrinkles

Not long after my "sister" moved out, my mom let me get a pug from the local shelter and I named him Wrinkles. Wrinkles was very naughty, which is probably why he cost only $20. He was abused at his old home so he had a lot of trauma, which I guess made him poop everywhere. And since my mom worked full time, he was stuck in a crate for extended periods of times, pooping all over it, and then he would eat his own poop. Poor Wrinkles.

After about five months of having dear Wrinkles, I went back over to my mom's after a long week at my dad's and Wrinkles was nowhere to be found. I asked my mom where he was and she told me to go upstairs and check my bed. And there it was, a BRAND-NEW First-Generation iPod Video on my pillow. It cost three-hundred dollars at the time, so wow, big deal. I could finally watch my favorite music videos on repeat! I was psyched! But then I noticed that Wrinkles was gone. That excitement quickly turned to grief. I watched the "Beautiful Liar" music video while crying at least forty times that night.

Why did everything I love have to be taken away from me? It just felt so *confusing*. And being confused like that, more than once, really effects a young girl. No wonder abandonment issues are what keep me up most nights.

And then there was the time my dad threw away all of my favorite Abercrombie and Limited Too clothes and made me wear only Walmart to school so he didn't have a "spoiled brat" as a daughter. For a young fashionista, that was the worst thing that could've happen. I am still traumatized from the rage he had that day.

Also, what the fuck?

My Dad Wears A MAGA Hat :(

My father (yes, we are going straight to father) can be a challenging man. He was the youngest of ten siblings and they all grew up on a dairy farm in central Pennsylvania working as a family business. We would go to visit my father's side of the family once a year when I was growing up and I swear it felt like we were entering an alternate universe. His childhood was night and day compared to mine.

I am a farmer's daughter.

When I was growing up, I hated how many chores my father would have us do. There was a list waiting for us after school every day. We also had to get up early for either summer camp or before school care, since he and my stepmom had to get to work in the city. It's safe to say I complained... a lot. He would always combat me with, "I was up at 5 a.m. every morning milking the cows!" And I was like, "Okay, but I don't see any cows here?" Haha, we fought... a lot.

Everything he did as a child was "work," so I guess it felt wrong for him to have kids that weren't constantly "working." We were always fucking working. Before, I hated him for the way we lived, but now, I guess I appreciate him for it. (Still a bit salty though.)

It's strange how once you grow up you see your childhood though a different lens. Also, I can't imagine what it must have been like to get up every morning and have to milk a cow. I would literally throw up. And be so pissed. It's funny because I am extremely allergic to dairy, wonder why? I bet he didn't even milk any damn cows — that liar!

My father was the only one in his family to go to a four-year university, and he ended up having a rather successful career in health insurance sales. He has a mindset that was built to be a worker. The way that his family operated was as a business, so I guess he tried to run ours like one too. It didn't work though because we were literally in a middle-class suburb and he worked in a high rise building downtown. No dairy farms in site.

All grievances aside, I do believe that his work ethic and mindset set my brothers and me up for success. But this "success" also came with a shit ton of other issues. For me, it is feeling like I am never doing or accomplishing enough. My self-worth is horrific at times because of some of the things my father said to me. The strong lack of emotional support from a young age fucked me up. You can't be a boss *and* a loving compassionate father at the same, and my father chose to be a boss.

Back to the chores — if we did not complete them "correctly," we would be verbally annihilated. My father would go around with his finger after we were done cleaning and if he found a speck of dust we would get yelled at and have to do it again. He is a perfectionist, or maybe he just has raging OCD. I definitely get some of that from him.

It was hard growing up with him. I resented him and always wanted a different type of parent. My parents were nothing like my friend's, neither was my home. That's what made growing up so hard. It was just very different. My parents were imposters in the suburb that we grew up in. They had years and years of conditioning that worked in an environment different than the one they raised their family in, and I think there's a lot of challenge in that. Only now are we all unraveling it all. I also think they drank so much to make themselves fit in. It was always "work hard, play hard," and the playing always involved a drink in hand. At least that's what I remember, and I tend to usually have a pretty good memory — despite the blackouts, lol.

Daddy Issues

My dad (sure, let's call him dad now) is my most challenging mentor. And I would be lying if I didn't say that there were times, if not years, where I did not like him. But like they say, you don't have to like someone to learn from them.

My dad taught me to be tough. Well, truth is, he would just beat me down mentally to the point where I would go run away and get belligerently drunk every weekend. But then he did teach me to always get back up, and no matter what, to always take the high road. Usually, the high road was the best option, but sometimes I do really wish I would have just let some people *have it*. The high road leads to a very blocked throat chakra, that's for damn sure. But none of this was easy to comprehend during my teens. And at the end of the day, what I needed was a present mom and a loving father. Neither were in sight.

Sometimes I wish I had a dad that raised me to feel overly loved, protected, and whole. One that made me feel seen and like I was a pretty little princess, but that just wasn't my upbringing. I had to work for what I wanted, no matter what. Sure, there are some good things that came out of having a wannabe military sergeant as a father. He taught me to never let bullshit slide, especially when it comes to business. He taught me to be highly productive, maybe to the point of giving myself anxiety attacks every day until I was medicated, but still, successful skills. I think in his head he was protecting me, specifically from being lazy and broke. And from having to be a housewife. I will never be a housewife; it's just not in my DNA. (Nothing against housewives. I love housewives, especially the New Jersey ones.) I just never had a "stay at home mom," so I can't really comprehend ever being one. I grew up around workers. White-collar workers that loved to fucking party.

My dad and I's relationship is better now. We still fight and bicker like hell, but it is all out of love. And we only ever bicker about work, money, and politics — but we will **not** go there right now. In our personal lives we don't argue anymore, and that is healthy for the both of us. He was always just doing his best. And like they say, the apple does not fall far from the tree. I truly am my father's daughter.

Fun fact: I used to lie to my dad in college and tell him I needed money for running shoes when, really, I needed it for alcohol. I was 40 pounds overweight; I was not running. Also, who needs three pairs of ASICS running shoes in an eight-month period? That man paid for all of my Cherry Admiral Nelson and Pineapple Burnetts. Ha, payback.

Healing

I have screamed at both of my parents at the top of my lung's countless times by now. Sure, not the best approach, especially when drunk as hell, but for some reason it always made us closer. That is love. So, maybe try that to start your healing. Yell at those motherfuckers and tell them how you really feel! Sorry, mom and dad, if you are reading this, I am a dramatic theatrical diva at heart — *we know this*. And the worst fights always involved liquor in our systems. We will never have *those* fights again.

I am grateful for my childhood even though it was extremely painful and lonely at times. But aren't all of ours? And hey, without those experiences I would not be sitting here writing this book. It all happened for a reason. My parents did a good job even if for years I was screaming about how much I hated them. What they did was force me to find the strength within myself, and that knowledge will never be taken. Ever. I can definitely say that I did not enjoy being a teenager. That shit almost killed me. So, if you are a teenager reading this, please know it gets better. It truly does. Once you're the shot caller, everything changes.

It is never a parent's intention to give us trauma, it just happens. Parenting is something I do not know yet, but I do know that my parents tried. My family went from being something that I ran away from, to something that I am now coming back to and appreciating on a whole different level. My family is powerful. There is history in our bloodline. My father is Croatian, and my mother's side is Czechoslovakian and Italian. Those Eastern Europeans are some strong-minded motherfuckers. There is a reason that I am the way that I am. There is a reason I am as tough as I am. There is a reason I am intelligent and think the way I do. It is because of my parents and all of my ancestors that came before them, mentally ill and *all*.

Fun fact: Without alcohol, most of my childhood trauma would never have happened. What a wild truth that is.

A Pennsylvania Girl's Heart

I used to hate Pennsylvania, but I was wrong for that. I am a Pennsylvania girl to the core, and *Pennsylvania* is a powerful place.

What I really hated was all the bad things that happened to me there. I ran to Colorado at eighteen with the sure decision that I would never return home.

I was going to run away for good and leave all the experiences that I had right there! HA. If only that worked out.

Pennsylvania was not the issue, I was. And bad memories follow you. You can't bury your entire past, *sorry*. You have to face it. But I didn't know that at eighteen. I was just so fucking mad all the time, so I needed to leave. I had shit to deal with away from Pennsylvania soil. I left to find myself. I left to heal. It's just funny because my behaviors didn't magically change once I got to Colorado or Atlanta. Nothing changed until I put down the alcohol. And that's when I realized that being from Pennsylvania is a cool thing and that it is my home. And powerful fucking people come from Pennsylvania.

I've had like ten adoptive families over the years. There were times when I just needed to escape my own, which was usually pretty easy to do because mine wasn't even around. It is also probably why I mesh well with all different types of people. I have spent a lot of intimate time with a lot of different families. Some people find it sad that I never felt like I had a home, but experiencing different types of home life made me who I am today, it made me different, and it made me one hell of a homemaker. Everywhere I go now feels like home. I am my own home.

Also, before anyone judges my parents or their own, I also need to mention that mine, all three of them, raised four of the most amazing people that I know. So, clearly, they did something right. They just had flaws and struggled in certain aspects, like any of us. We are all only human anyway.

I understand why my dad struggled to parent me, especially in my teenage years. First off, I was developed, difficult, and I loved to fucking party. I was also smart and usually ten steps ahead of him (as he likes to tell me now). And up until I was fourteen, my dad and stepmom only had kids every other week. They were like 50% parents. That honestly sounds like a pretty good deal, until it wasn't.

It was the same year when both my mom and my stepbrother's dad lost themselves to addiction and couldn't provide a place for us to stay every other week. So, we all had to move in full time with my dad and stepmom. That was a lot of change and responsibility put on them. Most parents were used to having kids full time, but they weren't, so I could see how that was not an easy change to adjust to. Especially as a newer couple without kids together that loved to fucking party. No wonder they left us every weekend to go to the lake house. Again, not making excuses, but as an adult now reflecting back, it makes sense... I guess.

My childhood lacked stability. It also lacked protection. I never felt fully protected. Not until I built it for myself. My apartment in Atlanta is truly the first place that has felt like home. My college living situations were close, but that was college, which is unstable in so many other ways. But this? This is a home that I created for myself. Well, my ex technically found the apartment, but it's mine now. This apartment is where I changed, so greatly. I needed it.

What I know now is that my family tried to make addiction and overall issues in the house seem less serious than they actually were. Most families do this. I am not sure why. Maybe it's because Boomers just love to hide the truth. So, I did the same with my drinking. I hid the seriousness of it from everyone. But I can promise you, hiding made it worse. So much worse. "*You are only as sick as your secrets,*" as my dear friend Sheryl says. Gosh, I wish I knew that back then.

Okay, back to my mom (I am all over the place with this one y'all). I wrote the following essay for college applications and scholarships when I was seventeen. Please enjoy and do not judge my mother. I love her! Sure, she caused me some trauma. But don't they all?

LEMONS — 2014

They say when life gives you lemons, make lemonade. I say when life gives you lemons, enjoy eating them.

"You have saved my life." When those words came out of my mother's mouth, I finally knew that what I was doing was just what she needed. A feeling of accomplishment came over me and I felt as if I could do anything. Knowing that my words and actions made someone so important to me make drastic changes in their life filled me with more than happiness. She was going to fight, enter rehab, and beat this thing. And my mother was thanking me.

The sun still shines. The lemons are still sweet. Why look at all the negatives with a magnifying glass when there are still many positives to be happy about in life. A strong person does not let life beat her down. I believe myself to be a strong person. Unlike many of my friends, I knew that my life at home differed from theirs. The divorce happened years ago. That was nothing. Living with my mom alone, was something. After she lost her job, I stood by her, helping her see the positives in her life. Knowing that it kept her on her feet for as long as it did, showed me that what I say to and do for people can make a difference. I have always been told "Elli, you always help me see the bright side of things" or "Elli, how do you do it—how are you so strong?" Some people live in a world where they think everything is perfect. Wanting to live in that perfect world is natural. I have learned that anyone can have that world, you just have to invent it for yourself.

My early years of growing up were not out of the ordinary, but when the trouble started, I knew I needed to step up and become the adult. From being home alone, making myself dinner and finding as many rides as I could on a day-to-day basis, I never allowed myself to get beaten down. So much good is out there in life and that's what we should be searching for.

I know that everyday can be sunny. Through the look in my mother's eyes every time I see her, I know that she admires me for all that I have done for her. I feel good when she looks at me that way. If I had never sat her down and told her to get her life together and to get help, there is a possibility that she would not be here with me today. Talk about a good feeling! I wish I could empower the minds of every teenager going through a rough time at home. It can get better, but in order for that to happen, someone has to step up and be the adult. This step was not easy for me, but when I decided to take it, I knew I was positively changing my life and the life of the ones around me. I never punished my mother in any way for what I have been through with her. This is because I know it is what made me who I am today. It gave me the opportunity to grow up, become independent and get smart.

I don't get nervous about meeting new people. Through traveling to rehab centers and reaching out to my relatives, I have learned to use those around me for help. My mother's illness, and alcoholism is an illness, taught me not to look at all the small things in life with a magnifying glass. Helping my mother to become and stay sober and to see the positives in her life while taking care of myself is one of my greatest accomplishments and gives me the power to see the positives in my life.

Elli Rose Cikovic

Awe, poor little Elli. It's funny because I was definitely a full-blown blackout artist myself by this point. (There are just some things that the college admission offices didn't need to know.)

P.S. I was accepted into all the schools that I applied for with this #slay.

16

Steelers Training Camp

My mom has always had a few *contacts* in the sports industry, particularly the Steelers.

When I was a senior in high school, she got me a pass to go with one of her friends to the team's pre-season training camp. I was hype, but obviously not hype enough to refrain from using my fake ID on the South Side the night before. And I got hammered, per usual. If you have been to Pittsburgh and were lucky enough to party on the South Side before Covid-19 ruined it, then you understand the atmosphere I am describing. Mario's and The Flats just hit different with a fake ID.

I woke up so hungover at my mom's apartment, but still, I was going to get my ass to the Steelers Training Camp for the day in hopes to meet my husband, *obviously*. But this hangover was bad. Brutal. Then, all of a sudden, I was no longer sitting at my moms, but in a retired player's basement waiting for my ride to get there and I was just staring at this... eyeless dog? A Pitbull with one eye I believe, yes. Poor guy. I must have still been drunk because I don't even remember how I got there, but it was a damn well recognizable jersey hanging on the wall, and I was somehow dressed and ready to go. Well, as ready as one can be when they blacked out the night before.

Once my ride got there, the player's cousin, he could tell that something was wrong, but we were running late so I told him I was good to go. I lied. Five minutes into the ride he had to pull over so I could throw up all over the side of the road. We had another thirty minutes to go and both knew fully well that I would not make it another minute without vomiting again. He turned around and dropped my ass right back off at my car.

No rookie husband for me. Alcohol blocked all my blessings.

Also, early morning hangover driving is still drunk driving. I was *lucky*.

Extra Story: Dicks On My Face

It was the first big party my senior year of high school and all of my friends and classmates were going to be attending. I made plans with a group of my closer girlfriends to get ready at the house that was closest to where the party was being held — fortunately, walking distance this time. When getting ready, we started to pregame and (of course) I took the pregame a little too far, which was not a rare occurrence for me. I remember being at the party and having a somewhat good time and then.... *blackout*.

When I woke up, I was on a couch in the middle of some random room in this guy's basement — brutally hungover and definitely about to throw up. I was supposed to make it back to my friend's house to sleep where my car was parked, but that didn't happen, which was also not a rare occurrence for me. I was scared and confused when I woke up, so I gathered my belongings, walked around all the other bodies passed out on the floor, and made my way out the back door. But first I needed to go to the bathroom, and when I looked in the mirror... I saw that there were dicks drawn all over my face... and body. Not a good feeling.

Fun fact: The guy who was hosting the party's parents were out of town and his grandma was watching him that weekend. His grandma was deaf. He literally threw a massive party in the basement while she was sitting upstairs in the living watching TV and had absolutely no idea. Classic.

Back to the story. So, I made my walk of shame down the street through this highly upper-class neighborhood. None of my friends were answering their phones and I knew they were either still sleeping or pissed at me. They were always pissed at me when I got too drunk, but I needed my keys and they were inside of my friend's house. Since no one was answering, I said fuck it and rang the front doorbell, with the dicks on my face. Luckily it was my friend who lived at the house that answered and she moved quickly to get me my keys and get me the fuck out of there before her parents saw. I felt sad. These moments were never fun, everyone dismissing me. I get it, trust me, but I really needed some fucking help in those moments.

I was living with my dad full time in a neighborhood not far away, but there was no chance in hell that I was going to show up there looking how I did. Luckily, by this point my mom had her own apartment on the North Side of Pittsburgh, so I texted my dad and said I was going and grabbing breakfast with her. I got in my car, brutally ill, and started to make my way to the city. I wasn't even five minutes into the drive when I had to pull over to throw up. And unfortunately, the only place to pull over was in a church parking lot. So, yes, I threw up outside of my car in a church parking lot with dicks all over my face.

After the quick vomit sesh, I gathered what little energy I had and got back in the car to finish out the drive. Luckily, I made it safely to my mom's apartment. Also, wow, I guess I did drive drunk more than I thought. I was not sober at that moment, so again, *lucky*. When I got to my moms, she opened the door and I just started to cry. She held me for hours and wiped all the dicks off my face. We never talked about it again. I love you, Mom.

So, ya, that was a rough one. And a week later that same group of girlfriends that I went to the party with hosted my first intervention at the local Starbucks. That was also not fun. They told me that at the party I passed out in a chair and threw up all over it. Then they showed me a picture of myself in thus chair, which was a terrifying sight. I promised them I would not blackout anymore, but that was a LIE. By the end of the year, I was banned from attending all parties with them. I literally got so drunk and ran two miles away at the last party before my ban, so I can't really blame them. But fuck, I needed some serious help. Also, fuck high school.

17

Addiction Tends to Be Genetic

Genetics play a major role in our habits, personality, and addictions. It is important to understand yours so you can be easier on yourself and, you know, maybe cut some things out that don't work so well for ya.

Addiction is a gift, in a way. It has taught me that I am not perfect. Point blank. It has also helped me understand and love others on a much deeper level. The research is simple: no one is perfect. However, I don't think I would be able to accept this without the pain and trauma that I have experienced myself *and* inherited from generations before.

A lot of people in my life struggle with addiction. Seems like almost everyone I love does in a way. So, I wonder, why is that exactly?

Well, I have come to conclusion that addiction is in my DNA so not only do I share it in my bloodline, but I also attract it. I believe that we attract those with similar DNA, such as friends, partners, co-workers, etc. And then there is just the cold hard proof that addiction runs in my immediate family — depression, panic disorder, anxiety, OCD, and ADHD do too. These "disorders" do not mean that there is anything wrong with us, or that we are bad people, it's just the truth of our genetic situation. We are a mental fuck fest. Kidding! We are a super intelligent and beautiful... *mental fuck fest.*

High intellect and addiction seem to always dance together. It's not a coincidence that most addicts are, or were at some point, known as the "best at something." What makes a "great" alcoholic also makes a great professor, actor, world leader, doctor, writer, painter, you name it. Addicts are usually "full senders," meaning they do the shit that they say they are going to do all the way, good or bad. And these are truly my favorite kind of people. I wish I could kidnap all the addicts I love and lock them in my apartment with me and keep them away from their vices. But that's just not possible, or is it? Haha.

The genetic addiction that I inherited is alcoholism (AUD). It is an *inherited* chronic brain disease. But this disease is different than most because of its symptoms. Why? Well, because its symptoms look like *bad behavio*r. Let me rant...

Lying is a symptom of AUD. Drinking yourself to sickness is a symptom of AUD. Blackout sex is a symptom of AUD. Drunk driving is a symptom of AUD. And I repeat: AUD is a brain disease, so there will be symptoms. What makes AUD so hard to cure is that unlike other diseases, it does not ignite symptoms that can be proven, because they always look like *bad behavior*. That's why you feel like a bad person after a bad blackout, because to most, you are. But the truth is that it's not *really* your fault — it's your addiction. And those horrible decisions you make while deep in the darkness of drunkenness are also not your fault. But it is your responsibility to stop them. And for me, the only way to do so was to quit drinking completely. There was no "in-between," and there never will be.

Addiction is not my fault, but it is my responsibility.

I wish there was a pill we could take to get rid of the symptoms of AUD, but there's not. Which is why it's so fucking hard to overcome. I just want to snap my figures and create a magical shot that gets rid of them all, but I can't, and that is why this disease is so fucking controversial.

What is said or done during a blackout is not personal nor vindictive, it is uncontrollable and impulsive. When you blackout you lose complete control, but you look conscious (kind of) even though you are really "lights out, no one is home." And then (cherry on top) you wake up and don't remember a thing. And sometimes what you don't remember is sex, which is the most intimate connection. And to do this over and over, every weekend, sometimes every day? Can you think of anything more horrible? And to live like that as a full-grown adult with real responsibilities, like kids? Madness. You can literally kill someone blacked out and not remember it, but have to spend the rest of your life in jail. You could also accidentally kill yourself. And to not remember something of this magnitude because of some evil magic liquid? Insanity.

AUD is a severe illness. It is serious enough to make people risk their lives and freedom every day. Every single fucking day. You would have to be sick. Which is why, again, AUD is a **chronic brain disease**. And it's usually fucking inherited. P.S. Still not a doctor or scientist. This is a *diary*. ☺

Alcohol affected every aspect of my life with a big portion of that being how I felt about my family. Going back and understanding my family history with addiction made it easier for me to quit. It also made it easier to love where I come from. This is my blood running through my veins, so I should love it, right? And I have this blood because two people decided to give birth to me. So, the issues I have I had to get it from somewhere, right?

Addiction makes you different, not damaged. Plus, especially now, modern medicine and research can help us live happier and healthier lives, a privilege most of our ancestors did not have.

I really do miss drinking less and less the more that I go without it. And that's something, right? Think about it, if you wanted to run away from a burning building what makes you think it's a good idea to turn around and run right back into the fire? That would be fucking stupid. I was an alcoholic by the time I was fourteen. You can't feed something that has done so much damage to you and your family for decades. Again, that is insanity.

Do some family research if you can, it helps. At least it did for me. I was a victim. Many of us are. Doesn't mean you have to die as one.

My dear friend, Sheryl, gave me some great insight on addiction. She said, "Addiction is the avoidance of self. Addiction is something that you do repeatedly even though you do not like the outcome. And that is PTSD." I found that interesting. She said that Bruce Lipton might have said this first, so to not quote her on it (which I still did), but it's not wrong. I haven't done my full research on Bruce or this concept, but hearing her talk about it made something click in my head.

Since DNA and environmental experiences lead to our addictions and traumas, and DNA adapts based on environment, then that means we can also un-adapt it, aka reprogram our DNA, aka get rid of shitty habits that feed our addictions.

It is also said that the foundation of trauma happens between the ages of 0-9. So, if we have to "please" our parents in that age range, that's probably why a lot of us feel the need to "people please." It is a trauma response. I went through my parent's divorce at age four, so that is where a lot of my initial child-parent dynamic issues started, like the lack of stability. And I know for damn sure that I am not the only one with this narrative. What I am saying is that no matter the trauma responses we initially learned, we are able to reverse them. We are able to get better. We are able to reprogram our DNA.

Sure, I don't know all of this for definite, but one thing I do know is that since I cut out alcohol... my brain works differently. My natural serotonin is back, and I feel *real* happiness. I feel freedom. I feel like I finally have control over my life again. So yes, my DNA and habits have absolutely been reformed. And the only thing I can compare this feeling to is *magic.*

I tried countless times to break my addiction to alcohol before succeeding. I always wanted to quit, I just never thought it would be possible. That is until I started to test out something that I like to call "cycle break zones." (Yes, I made this concept up.)

Cycle Break Zones

1. **72-hour zone** = get your fucking shit together

2. **7-day zone** = habit break zone

3. **30-day zone** = chemical break zone

Let me break this down.

I did countless 72-hour break zone attempts, which I usually succeeded in. Three days is easy, considering I was usually hungover half the time, wallowing away in my despair.

The 7-day zone is where it started to get tricky. I don't recall many times making it seven days without drinking over my ten-ish years. But what I do recall is feeling really fucking good when I did. But once the weekend rolled around, I had to drink. It was too hard not to. There was no other option.

And for the 30-day zone... welp, I never did that. The only time I did was in 2022 when I quit for good.

This cycle-zone concept helped me. It helped me to have something to work at, even though I usually failed. I guess this is where the bridge between science and spirit meet. I was spiritually ready to quit when I did. All I can really say here is that what is right for you will feel right. Our intuition is strong, listen to it.

There are loads of ways to face addiction breaking, and I believe these tactics can be used on other addictions as well. For example, going thirty days without sex, caffeine, or weed. Whatever you feel you need a break from, I say try it. Sure, you may fail, but there is so much growth in *failing*.

Also, I know that all of my addictions are not broken yet and I will definitely have to use this tactic again in my life. Addiction leaks into every part of my life, which means I need to be aware, overly aware. The work will never stop for me. It can't.

Cycle break zones worked for me because they gave me a goal. I didn't even know what I was doing half the time, but something just told me to keep trying.

It might sound strange, or even unbelievable to some, but there are some things that I just know I need to do. They come from a higher power, I don't know exactly how, but I know the messages are real. I have been receiving messages my whole life, telling me to keep going and to keep trying. And that I did.

This is why I needed to write this book; I need to share this miraculous thing(s) that happened to me all from just finally *listening*. And doing research. Do your fucking research.

18

Forensics Tournament 2012

During the winter of 2023, I found recordings of myself practicing an essay I wrote on depression in 2012. I had no idea that these recordings still existed until I was about 70% done with the first draft of this book — talk about a pleasant surprise. This was a very pivotal moment for me because after I listened to these recordings, I realized that I have been doing exactly what I am doing *now* for over a decade. I take my pain and heal it through writing, with the intent to share my knowledge with others to try and help them also heal. Call me... Mother Mary? Kidding!

After finding the recordings I did a deep dive into my email, which I have had since I was 13, and luckily found the written copies of it too. This essay was written in an Honors English class I took my sophomore year of high school with a teacher named Mr. B. He was known to be one of the hardest teachers at my school, but he loved me, I did well. And I was a good writer. He let me know I was a good writer. I would lock myself away for ten hours at a time and just go ham typing. His assignments were treacherous, the worst being his "RRJ's." For those assignments, we would have to read a book and write like 30 pages on it in some sort of format I can't even remember. I just remember it was hard and everyone dropped his class because of it, but not this chick.

For the essay I am about to share, we had the option to do another RRJ assignment or present a persuasive essay we did earlier in the year live at a Forensics Tournament — completely memorized.

Obviously, I took the choice that seemed like less work to me. I was going to present my persuasive essay on depression, that I wrote during a very dark period of my life, to a bunch of random nerdy kids. My fellow students all chose topics like robotics, political debate, and climate change. Guess I've never known how to fit in.

The tournament took place on a Saturday morning at a random high school. All participants were a combination of students from multiple different schools within my area. To put it frank, I did not match the crowd. My presentation was set to take place in a smaller classroom with about twenty competitors, and my teacher would be in there to support. At the time, I didn't have any professional clothing so I had to borrow one of my stepmom's button ups. I chose her hot pink one, of course, because what else screams *depression*? My stepmom is tiny and so the top fit a bit tight on my boobs, considering I was at least a 32D at the time — (birth control had my titties poppin').

Okay, it was my time to shine and I got up to present. I remember it being the ass crack of dawn too, just to set the scene a little more. I was proud of my speech and it was exactly ten minutes, as I had spent all night in front of my dad and stepmom's bathroom mirror learning, recording, and timing it, hence the recordings that I found. Everything started off great. I was about to get through the first minute and a half and nail the thesis until... my shirt popped open like a piñata. Bra and tits *out*. I vividly remember getting frantic and turning around to try and button back up my shirt, and for a moment I thought about giving up, but damn, I did not want to have to write another 30-page paper, and in order to get the credit, you **had** to present. So, I said fuck it. I buttoned that shit up, *like a boss*, and turned back around to keep it pushin'. Gosh, it popped right when I opened my arms and said "depression!" all loud and proud, because that was the theme of the essay... depression. What a great combo... tits and depression. Sounds like my life.

Fuck it though because after that, I didn't drop a line. The presentation continued for another nine minutes, still fully memorized, and I got third place. Guess the tits helped.

That class is where I learned how to write. And clearly, it's where I learned to memorize and perform too. The more I revisit my past, the more I realize that I have been writing and acting my entire life. It is what I am meant to do. I am meant to experience things heavily and feel such deep-rooted pain in order to share it in a way that helps the world heal. That is my purpose.

Okay, back to the essay. Please bear with me, some of these facts do not fully line up. I was learning. And I was fifteen. Gosh, I can't believe I wrote and presented this live and to *that crowd*. I am very proud of that version of Elli.

Depression — 2012

Concept Statement: *The happiest face always hides the darkest secrets.*

Chad is just a normal guy living a normal life. But lately, he has not been feeling the same. He is stressed at work, his wife has recently become sick, and his teenage kids have gotten out of control. He doesn't feel right. Everything keeps getting worse. He does not want to continue. Chad is going to end his life all because of a feeling that he does not know how to control. Depression is a serious illness that numerous people face on a day-to-day basis. Okay, everyone feels depressed at times. But we need to recognize that for some people, it is far more serious, and they need our help. Depression needs to be taken seriously and we can do so by knowing what it is, what it does, and how it can be helped.

It is important to know the causes of depression so we can help depressed people, friends, and family understand how painful it is and why it is not possible to "snap out of it." There is no one simple answer to what depression is, but there are many psychological reasoning's and explanations that we should all know. The dictionary defines depression as "an emotional condition... characterized by feelings of hopelessness." There are many factors that play a part in depression. Everyone should know that people with family history to depression have a slightly higher chance to form it. It is important to know this so those with depressed relatives can be more careful. However, some people do hide their depression so well that no one will have a clue they were sad. So, we should be very aware of the people around us because even the happiest face may be hiding the saddest feelings. The Patriot Ledger, 1999 tells a story by Sue Scheibel about a young high school student named Ali. Ali's parents recently got divorced and she had to move away to a new school with her dad. She was not making friends at this school; she was even getting bullied by the "popular girls" and eventually stopped going. She was lost in her feelings. Ali began harming herself thinking that it would be the only way to ease the pain. Soon it was not helping enough, and on New Year's Eve when she wasn't invited to any party and had nothing to do, she decided to give up. Ali swallowed 60 tablets of an over-the-counter pain killer. She didn't tell anyone, but luckily her dad sensed something was wrong and immediately called for help. Ali lived at the hospital for four days. She was diagnosed with clinical depression just like her mom. Over the next years thoughts of ending her life still came to mind. People like Ali are lucky that they had someone there for them. We all need to be capable of helping someone just like Ali's father. It is situations like these that trigger depression, and we need to recognize that our help and support can save lives. There are 3 types of depression that we should all understand. The first is called Bipolar disorder, then Dysthymia, and lastly, the most severe, known as Major or Clinical Depression. Major depression cannot be triggered by one specific event, but like Ali for an example, it's not very hard to gather up the smaller events that lead to it. We all need to be aware of the different types of depressions because the more we know, the more we can help. The book, Depressive Disorders, states that the Global Burden of Disease study conducted by Harvard, said that major depression causes more of a burden on people and society than most other illnesses. This is just one example to why our society needs to understand how serious depression is. A depression survivor named Julie-Anne wrote an analogy in her autobiography called Nothing but Respect. She stated, "Cars take certain things to run properly. They need gas, oil, anti-freeze, and more. Without these items, the car would not run. The human brain is the same way. Sometimes, without the formation of the essential chemicals the brain will not work properly. Depression is one of these times, and if we are all aware of the many factors that play a role in depression, then we will be able to help."

Though there is much information about this illness, most of us refuse to listen to it, and we continue on, making matters worse and worse. The book Straight Talk about Anxiety and Depression states, "One of the characteristics of depression is the feeling that things have always been bad, and they always will be, the inability to imagine any other feeling than the feeling of being depressed. In those few low moments when it seems that life will never get better, suicide may come to seem like a solution." Depression can affect a person's mind as much as their body. Say someone my age is depressed; they are more likely to get in forms of trouble such as bad grades, stealing, or even running away. However, we need to know that depression can affect anyone, no matter what age. Some people will become very irritable, they may abuse drugs and alcohol, they may lose or gain weight, and the most serious of all, they may commit suicide. Let me explain with a story... there is a 15-year-old girl who was a good student and had many friends, one including a boyfriend of 2 years. But, once she found out that her boyfriend was sneaking around with her best friend, she changed completely. She could not cope and ending up cutting all connections with friends and family. A week later, she couldn't handle it anymore and committed suicide. Imagine the worst physical pain you've ever had, maybe a broken leg, toothache, or surgery. Now, multiply that by ten and take away the cause. That is the pain that depression brings on people. Many depressed individuals feel there is no way to end the misery and torture of depression other than committing suicide. More than 5,000 people my own age commit suicide every year. That is a big number, no one should feel that way, especially that many. It is just another reason why we need to recognize how serious depression is, and we can't hide from the fact that it needs to be addressed. Say you're watching TV; it is bright and you are happy. Then, you turn off the lights. It is now dark; you are uncomfortable, and blinded. Soon you will become used to this and start walking around, running into walls, and tripping over toys. You have so many problems and you do not want to turn on the lights to face them. You don't want to leave your depression, you are comfortable. But, one day, you must flick the switch. This is what we need to do; we need to help them flick the switch! Depression may end fatally, but there are always options that we can give those to help recover and fight on from this serious illness.

When someone is depressed, they lose responsibly for their lives, let alone their sickness. There are many ways to cope, and we need to be aware of them so that we can help. Recovering from depression does mean that a person has to take responsibility for their own life but help from others never hurts. In 2008, the famous Harry Potter writer, JK Rowling shared her story of suffering from depression with Fox News. Rowling suffered with suicidal thoughts after separating from her husband and being homeless during her mid-twenties. Rowling said that her daughter is what made her get help. Her daughter grounded her by making her realize that she needs to keep in touch with what is important in life. Continual therapy got her back up on her feet. She continued fighting and ended up selling more than 400 million copies of her Harry Potter series and creating a billion-dollar industry. There is always a way to fight through depression. The understanding and support of family can be a great coping mechanism alone. We can do this; we have to give our support to our friends and family in need. There are also many basic ways to try and recover from depression such as exercise, diet, or even sleep. So why not put on your running shoes and take that person for a run. Some more include improving your surroundings, therapy, or just simply talking to someone. If we do this for each other, the results will be well worth it. There are many different options, and we need to look at them individually so we can take depression piece by piece and help those in need fight it. There are also Antidepressant drugs, which are the most common approach to treating depression. We need to encourage friends and family to see the doctor and get these medicines if they need it. The 2009 edition of Psychology Today states, "To successfully cope with depression most people stumble onto their own combination of lifestyle adaption, therapeutic techniques, medications, and mental adjustments." This is not as hard as it has to be. Any one of us could save a life by helping out a depressed individual. Knowing and applying the coping skills to do so will help make a sickness free world.

Depression is a serious illness and we need to take it seriously because if left untreated can lead to death. Related back to Chad, people like him take their sadness to the point where they want to end their lives. Even famous people, such as JK Rowling, are suffering. Depression needs to be taken seriously and we can do this by understanding what it is, what it does, and how it is treated. Depression doesn't always win, there is always a way to defeat it, and we need to be there to stand by the sides of those in need.

Okay, it's a little concerning how much I talk about suicide in this, but to be frank, this was written right after the night I had to take my mom to the hospital because she was so fucked up. And when she was in the ER, I heard her tell my dad and the doctor that she was suicidal... for the first time. They sent her to the psych hospital that same night and then, *just like that*, I was living full-time with my dad. That was a horrible day. So yeah, makes sense.

This was my version of healing. Rather than hurting myself, I wrote about it. That makes sense to me. Writing is how I process and channel my feelings. I did, however, always get a hunch that Mr. B was concerned about me. He wasn't the only one.

My pain was real. Very real. And I felt so alone. I also still can't believe I talked so much death in a hot pink button up. And to that crowd?! Poor children. Just trying to have a good Saturday morning with their buds competing in debates about robots. But there I was, young Elli, sticking out like a sore thumb per usual, ready to flash them some tits and talk about suicide for ten minutes straight. Only now am I realizing how drastic this all was.

But back then, it was just another day.

19

Drinking & Depression

I have anxiety. I have depression. I have abandonment issues. I have an anxious attachment style. I have high functioning alcoholism (AUD) and binge drinking disorder. I have an addictive personality. And I really do think I have OCD, at least a little. (Probably more than a little.)

But these things do not control me, at least not anymore. Except for overthinking, if that can be considered a condition. I don't know how much overthinking is over-overthinking, but I think I do it.

My great grandmother was sent to get electric shock therapy (ECT) in the fifties to treat her depression. As I have mentioned before, many of my issues are genetic — especially depression. The majority of my family members struggle with depression, but *apparently* only around 5% of the world's adults have it. Guess we are just one of the higher contributors. There's no way it is only 5% though, right?

The Cloud

Every so often, I get this feeling. It's as if a dark cloud comes over me and fills up my body, mostly the stomach area, with... darkness. I am just flooded with these bad memories and feelings of shame and discomfort. My first thought usually goes, "I don't feel good." And then, "Fuck I am disgusting." And then, "I need to get up and do something because if I'm not doing something at all times then I am not working hard enough and therefore I am a failure and will fucking die, sad and depressed."

Intense, I know. I'm not done. Then my root and sacral (chakra) areas feel like they are being attacked directly by that gray cloud of regret and shame from years of invasion and lack of safety, and I just feel gross, and then stuck. So stuck. Most of my shame and guilt stems from sexual trauma. It's obvious, right?

Sure, I have always been a rather horny gal, which is probably a contributing factor as to why I got myself into so many dicey situations while fucked up, but still… there is pain. The good thing is I am working through it now, not suppressing and adding to it. Also, please note that no matter what happened, I still find sexuality empowering, strong, and beautiful. Owning my sexuality is important to me. That's why not having power over it for ten years affected me so greatly, and still does.

In 2021, I spent three months working with a holistic intimacy healer named Hanna Dylan (@hanna_dylan_). She taught me ways to work through the energy of past sexual traumas. One of my favorite tools that I learned from her is a self-care ritual called *mirror work.* When doing mirror work you can either be naked or clothed, being naked makes it more intense. What you do is you sit in front of a mirror and look at yourself naked (or whatever you choose) for at least ten minutes, no distractions. You look deep into your own eyes and ask questions like: *What do I see? What am I avoiding? How can I love myself more? Who do I get to be to step into my next level? What about my body do I love? What do I not love so much?* Really you can ask yourself anything that feels right or comes up. The goal is to work on creating and nurturing that deeper connection with yourself. It is difficult, but with time it gets easier. Trust me, it's worth doing at least once.

A lot of my time now is spent working on myself, aka "self-healing." It's what helped me become strong enough to quit. The dark cloud I spoke about before, it still comes. But now it goes too. Like how the normal sky works. When drinking, it would come, but instead of leaving, it would just continue to grow, rapidly. It was *always* there. Always in the background, if not already in the forefront. Grayness constantly in my head. Blackouts would help me "shut" the cloud up. Well, at least I thought. What I was really doing was drowning it with loads of liquor, aka feeding it, which led to fake feelings of ease until I would get so drunk that it all stopped, which is... a blackout. And then I would wake up with even more shame and regret to face — a bigger, stronger, and denser cloud. I thought that this was going to be my life forever... but no. Turns out this self-healing shit actually works, and I needed it to quit. I needed it to destroy my cloud.

Anxiety

I have anxiety. Anxiety does not feel good. For me it involves excessive biting of the cheeks, constant overthinking, face picking, and restlessness. It used to be a lot worse. Quitting alcohol absolutely helped, but honestly it is still very prevalent in my life. I know I should probably say more on how much it changed after cutting out alcohol, but it didn't *change* much, it's just a lot less intense. Like a lot, a lot. My mental health issues did not magically disappear when I quit drinking, but they sure are easier to manage.

I drank mostly to ease my anxiety, but it never went away until the blackout, which then led to me waking up in an even more anxious state. Because now not only am I already a naturally anxious girl, but I also have to try and figure out how I got to bed. Or if it wasn't my bed, figure out where the fuck I was, and sometimes — who the hell was lying next to me. Now that... that's the constant state of anxiety and depression I talk about. I was always terrified in those moments but would play it off as if it was normal. Because I guess it was normal for me, to an extent. And that is scary.

The good thing is that these scenarios will never happen again. *Phew.* I already feel better after writing that out. Nothing can make me as anxious again as waking up not remembering something I did... naked. No. Now, my anxiety is about my agent not emailing me back fast enough and thinking she hates me. That is normal anxiety, at least for an actor. Trying to figure out why your underwear is on backwards and you are covered in throw up is a different kind of anxiety. You can't shake that off with a walk and glass of kombucha, you just can't.

So, what I am saying is, yes, I have anxiety. Social anxiety too. Loads. It may not seem like it when you meet me, I hide it well, or at least I try. I'm an actress you know.

Therapy

I started going to therapy bi-weekly when I was fourteen, but that was not my first time sitting in a therapist office. My first time was when I was four — shortly following my parent's divorce. I remember looking into the office from the waiting room with my little prepubescent eyes and seeing my mom talking to the doctor, and then bringing me in for my assessment. I went in for a few sessions and all I can seem to remember is the candy. I loved the candy.

My emotions have always been heavy, even as a little girl. And I was taught at a young age that therapy was and **always** is an option. Therapy is an important part of my story because without it I am not sure where I would be. My therapist(s) were there when the adults in my life couldn't be, at least not how I needed them to be.

I learned various tips and tricks throughout my years of therapy that continue to help me get through dark and depressive feelings. I can now feel, name, and move through my feelings. These feelings have voices, voices telling me that I am not enough and not doing enough. Voices yelling at me in the mirror saying I'm not skinny enough or fit enough. Voices of regret and shame from the years of sexual trauma telling me I am used up. The cloud has *many* forms. But with the right tools and a clear head, I am able to work through these feelings rather than push them down. Well, I am trying at least. Again, still in my twenties.

When I was in high school, I had a long-term therapist tell me that I will most likely never face complete devastation when it comes to the death of a loved one. This broke my heart. *However*, what I think she meant was that no matter how close I get to someone or feel that I "need" them, I will always be able to handle their exit. She knew the depths of loneliness I faced during dark periods, all at such a young age. I didn't like hearing her say this because of how horrible it sounded, but maybe she was right. I formed a layer of comfort with being abandoned and left alone, and that's partially where grief stems from — the fear of being alone from the ones you love.

With age, I am getting softer and I think this "not needing anyone" cycle is breaking. I suppressed so many feelings for so long, and that caused a lot of distance with myself and others, something I am still working on today. To my loved ones, I promise I will be sad when you die. I honestly might have misinterpreted her. She told me this during a *very* dark session.

The cool thing about therapy is that you get to decide who you want to work with and when. I have had a few therapists over the years, and each one was very different. If you are interested in therapy, I recommend it. The hardest part is getting started. It gets easier as time goes on, I promise.

Guilt, Insecurity, and Disassociation

A lot has changed during my first two years being alcohol-free regarding my mental health. Specifically with three major deep-rooted feelings: *guilt, insecurity, and disassociation*.

Guilt is rare for me now. Gosh, I do not miss the daily guilt. Countless mornings of waking up in a panic trying to figure out what I did the night before. So many mornings wondering if I had sex or not. College was the worst of this. I would wake up wondering where I was, who I was with, and what I did. Did I say anything crazy? Who is this person texting me? Where is my jacket? My fucking underwear... AGAIN?!

To be overly honest, you could line-up probably twenty guys from high school and college that I have slept with and I would have no fucking clue who they are. This makes me sick to even think about, let alone write out. I was so easy to give my body away. And when the morning hit, I would be devastated. This feeling became "normal" to me by the time I was only sixteen years old. It is also not my intention to blame the guys here, but, I mean, I literally turn into a lifeless zombie when I blackout, so, I am sure they were not all *perfect* men. I was definitely taken advantage of some of the time, but again, I was doing it a lot. There is such a gray line when it comes to blacking out and sex. This is why I am writing this book to tell all y'all that if you blackout and do scary things, *MAYBE,* you just shouldn't drink. Okay?

Blacking out and doing shit I would never remember was very normal to me. I have been naked and *entered* by people who I don't even know. That is literally the worst possible scenario I could ever imagine today and it was literally happening to me only a few years ago. Wow. So yeah, probably why most of my guilt and shame is buried with those "memories." They are all somewhere deep in my subconscious mind.

Being *insecure* is rare for me since I quit drinking. Don't get me wrong, I still have insecure days about how I look, my weight, my finances, and my overall existence, but nothing like it used to be when I was drinking. My *real* confidence didn't come back until I quit. I am talking about that deep rooted security about who you are, what you do, and what you say. I am not perfect, but I am better than I was two years ago. I am secure in who I am as a person. I am secure about my decisions. I am secure about who I am becoming. No longer am I intentionally turning my brain off to "loosen up" and "say fuck it" and make decisions that I literally do not remember. I am intentional at all times now. I am present. And no one has the power to tell me something that I do not already know about myself.

The number of times I got, "Oh my god you were wild last night!" "Hey, are you okay today?" "Do you know what you said last night?" or "Holy shit you are such a good time, you love to party!" Ugh, too many to count. As a young girl with high anxiety, those were the worst things to hear. In high school, Mondays were scary. They were gossip central. And then really any day in college when walking around campus I would have an underlying fear of seeing someone who *maybe* saw me do something that I don't remember. Given, not everything that I did was bad, some of it was badass, but it's the principle of not knowing what I did that scared me. I didn't trust myself. I didn't want to be in my own skin.

It's as if I created my own personal hell. But guess what... I don't do that shit anymore.

Disassociation, specifically forced, is rare for me since I quit drinking. I no longer have a tool or quick escape mechanism to completely leave my body. Now, I have to be in it, more than ever before. And honestly, I kind of love it. It took time to get here. And I really didn't expect the journey of getting to know myself again to be so beautiful — all while so brutally present. I am *present* now. I can't leave my body daily anymore. I feel a lot, I always have, and I am learning to like (maybe love) it. I just wasn't strong enough to feel it all before.

Running

She a runner she a track starrr. Yeah, that's me. I am a runner, always have been. Well... I was. I ran. Ran from home, ran from my family, ran from my darkness, ran from my truth, and really just ran from anything I could fucking get away from. I even ran from some of my most valuable female friendships, some of whom I am still working to repair today. I was just so lost during my darker years, always leaving a piece of my soul behind.

I ran from Pittsburgh to Colorado at eighteen, without knowing a single person there. I ran from Colorado to Atlanta, knowing only two people this time. I even ran from myself, for years. I was left, so therefore I would leave too, even my own body at times. That was my conditioning.

Truthfully, I was trying to run away from my sadness and depression, thinking that that's how you get rid of it. And how I ran was I chased it all down with a bottle. It took just one year of alcohol sobriety to have a full 180 shift and see that I don't have to run anymore. I can instead — *decide*.

My fogged lens is now off. Those daily guilt trips and self-hatred... gone. It has not been an overnight journey and it's still not over, but there are powerful changes happening in my life that I know would not be possible if I was still drinking. The truth is — running does not solve your problems, but sometimes it does get you closer to the real solution, which is usually within yourself. At least that's been my experience this far. The places that I ran to brought me home... to myself. So, I guess it all happened for a reason. Maybe I still am a runner, but instead of running away, I am running *to*. Now that is power.

Three Months Sober: My Dark Thoughts (2022)

It is three months into my sobriety and I have started to *strongly* notice this anxious, deep feeling from inside. It's as if something in my body needs to release, and I just can't get to it.

Working out helps. Organizing, cleaning, talking to friends, walking, stretching, puzzles, they all help... to an extent. But nothing gives me that deep release I am craving. The best way I can describe it is as an irritating feeling inside of my skin and bones, maybe even in my blood, that needs to be released... through a vein. I believe this is the first time in my life where I've fully understood why people cut themselves.

Sorry if this is triggering for some, I am just being honest. Honest about my dark thoughts, and honest about how fucking hard it can be to live with depression.

For so many years I used drinking as a way to harm myself. Sex too. Sex can be a form of self-harm, if you haven't registered that yet. I know that for a fucking fact because I used it as such. I just could not stop. I couldn't stop the bingeing and the — bam — blackout — bam — sex with strangers. It just kept happening. Part of me feels like it felt good to hurt myself because it was the only thing that could get me that release that I needed, but really, I was just making the cut deeper.

I have to work hard to try to be happy. And by "work hard," I mean by keeping a routine and doing the things that my brain needs to feel the feelings of happiness, like sitting by my pool and going to my Pure Barre classes. Which also means I need to work hard to make money so I can afford to do such things. Damn, maybe being a nepo baby would have been easier, but honestly, probably not.

I believe I was capable of self-harming so much with alcohol and sex because I found a way to make it feel different every time — different party, different season, different drink, different boy, etc. I was able to manipulate my mind into believing that I was exploring and growing, never self-harming. However now, looking back, it all feels and looks a lot like fucking abuse. And that is a scary but truthful thought.

It is hard to be truly happy in the world we live in, but I have a real fucking shot at it without alcohol. So, I am going to do everything I can to live a happy life. I deserve it after all the shit I've been through. I know that it will take work. It's not like you quit drinking and *poof* everything is better with the snap of your fingers, but at least my chances are a lot higher now. I can work with that.

2024 Note: And two years later y'all, without any alcohol in my system, I am happy. It's not all perfect, and I still have bad days, but it's better than ever before. A lot better. I feel safe in my body. And I didn't know life could be so damn beautiful.

20

Freshman Year with Fiona

"Don't waste your crazy!" - Fiona Apple

When I moved to Colorado, I didn't know a single person that lived there. And I was so fucking excited about that. Well, "no one," except for this girl named Fiona. Yes, Fiona. Like in Shrek. I met Fiona off an app that Colorado State provided us to find our freshman year dorm-mate. Think Tinder, but for the person that you're going to be platonically sleeping next to for ten months. I wanted a random roommate, but not random to the point where we had absolutely nothing in common. Really, I had one requirement... someone that liked to fucking party.

And boy oh boy did I hit the jackpot.

I always knew that going to school far away from home was what I needed to do. Sure, it was not all sunshine and rainbows, but I got a fresh start. Which I needed *badly*. It was a place where no one knew about my past. No one knew about all the boys that I had slept with. No one knew about my weekly blackouts, at least not yet. No one knew shit. High school pretty much sucked and I always felt so alone, but once I met Fiona — everything changed.

Fiona is from Southern California. She is 100% authentically herself. And I loved every single thing about her before we even met.

When I first saw her profile on the roommate app, a few things stood out to me. First, she didn't seem to care what other people thought about her, which was a foreign concept to me at the time. Second, she was cool, like really fucking cool. And third, she liked to get drunk, *very drunk* — just like me! I immediately knew I had to have her as my roommate. Once she said yes, I was beyond excited to have her by my side and to be my partner in crime as we both took on a new state and our first year of college together.

The summer before heading to school, I went on my senior trip to good ole Ocean City, Maryland (can't seem to stay away) and one night I got really fucked up and spent the night with someone that I shouldn't have. I was so embarrassed when walking back to my condo from his and trust me, a walk of shame on the Ocean City, Maryland boardwalk is *extra* shameful, but this time my sorrow was a little different because now I had Fiona to call. And that felt really good.

She made me feel better. She totally understood me and we hadn't even met in person yet. Calling her made me feel heard and like I wasn't a waste. I also now knew I had an escape — I knew Colorado really was going to be different. Well, not different in the drinking department, but different in the female friendship department, which was what I needed so badly.

I could write an entire book on just my year living with Fiona. I swear we were chasing Cherry Admiral Nelson's back with a nice crisp Four Loko er'day. We assigned a specific drinking theme to each day of the week so we had a "reason" to get fucked up, as if we needed a reason — ha. That first week of school was liberating... from what I can remember.

Colorado changed my life for the better, *forever*. But there were still a lot of challenges. That first year is when I put on the most weight ever. My "freshman fifteen" was a freshman forty, easily. Mostly stemming from daily drinking, severe depression, abuse of antidepressants, eating dairy when I was clearly allergic, and the all-inclusive 24/hour food halls. My antidepressants were so fucked up back then. Blacking out every single night on medication like that is not good. And I hate to admit this, but sometimes when Fiona would wake up hungover and sad with me, I would give her some of my pills. I called them "happy pills" and pretty much forced her to take them. And then two hours later we would start binge drinking again. Yikes.

Fiona never made me feel bad about the fucked-up shit I would do. She actually did the complete opposite, which was something I was not used to in female friendships. She also kept me alive — not really sure how she was able to do that while also outdrinking me. The girl is a tank. A beautiful tank. However, there were also some nights when I would get really drunk and say mean things to her. I still get sick to my stomach thinking about those nights. I hated myself, not her. That's how that works. She was just the closest to blame.

It was also not *all* partying. Sure, we liked to party hard, but we also liked to work hard. Well, that's if you consider taking sixty milligrams of Vyvanse and pulling all-nighters in the library "working." We would crank out all our assignments for the semester in two days and then binge drink after to be able to fall sleep, aka *sedation*. The amount of Adderall and Vyvanse we consumed that year was concerning, but that's how we got shit done. Smarter not harder y'all, if you call that smart (haha help). Those were some of my favorite nights though. Staying up all night talking about our dreams and problems with boys, which that section took up most of the conversation, all while geeked out on Adderall. Those conversations ran deep. We told each other things that we had never told anyone before. That is when I truly fell in love with my friend Fiona.

I want to tell at least one story from that year, so I will share my favorite. It was a simple night. A night I didn't blackout. An "Elli & Fiona Night," as we liked to call them when we would go out partying just the two of us. The story goes as follows.

Circa 2015, Fiona and I were sitting in our three-hundred square foot dorm room. I looked over at her and said, "Hey, wanna get fucked up?" and she responded with a giant smile and said, "Yes." Always yes. God that felt good. We then, per usual, finessed a ride to the local Chinese liquor store where they accepted our horrific fake ID's and picked up a bottle of Cherry Admiral Nelsons along with two Four Loko's to chase. No wonder I put on so much weight that year — we drank that shit like water. I don't think I could even sniff Cherry Admirals now without throwing up. Yuck.

We decided to get drunk and go to one of the random houses behind our dorm. Those houses were always throwing parties and we would just walk over and enter them like it was nothing. People welcomed us everywhere that we went, no questions asked. We were magic together.

We were also little thieves. And this was the night when we acquired our most prized possession — *The Hanging Pineapple*. It was a beautiful seven-pound cemented pineapple that was hanging on the wall at one of the party houses. When we walked in, we spotted it immediately. I remember distracting someone and then Fiona reached up, grabbed it, and ran. I followed suit and we took that fucking pineapple right back to our room. It became our third roommate. And every time we would drink moving forward, we would cheers to the pineapple.

I am not sure why I chose this story as it is one of the mildest of them all. It's just one of my favorite memories with her. It was an innocent night, meaning I didn't blackout or fuck some random dude, and that felt good. It's also the fact that I hadn't found much true deep friendship until Fiona. This is not me saying that I don't have lifelong friendships from high school, it's just when Fiona looked at me, she didn't see a damaged responsibility because of my past. She saw a friend. A peer. It was just different. She saw the real me — the me *without* the eighteen years of trauma that I brought to that doorstep in 2015. She accepted me and loved me, no matter what. You can't replace that kind of feeling after coming from such a fucked-up situation. You just can't.

I grew up in an area that was stuck up, small minded, and judgmental as shit. It wasn't like that in Colorado. Everyone was just as wild and free-spirited as me. Even though I was still severely depressed my entire time there, I was happier than I had ever been in Pittsburgh. I needed to run from home to find myself, to find my people — and I did. Colorado saved me while almost killing me at the same time. I partied my heart out there and left most of it in piles on the street. I still have healing to do and I plan on going back to my college town eventually.

But I feel like I partially owe my life to that message I sent in 2015 on that damn roommate app. Fiona was my savior.

Fun fact: Fiona's main picture on the roommate app was of her smiling so creepily with blood pouring out of her nose. That's when I knew she was the one. I showed some of my high school friends the picture and they all were like, "What the fuck is she doing? She looks weird." I remember I looked at them and said, "She is amazing." I never belonged in that high school friend group. I feel like most of them just saw me as a drunk hoe who did embarrassing shit. Maybe I am wrong, but I really did feel like I was just a misplaced burden to them all. And that's a tough narrative to escape, even if it was only ever in my head.

I escaped that narrative when I left, I was able to just be Elli. Fiona is not the only best friend for life that I met in Colorado either. I was blessed with very powerful, life long female friendships from college.

And they are still some of my favorite people to this fucking day.

Freshman Year Letter: Attempting to Fight the Cops

I got so drunk my freshman year of college. Like almost kicked out of school drunk. Below is one of the letters I had to write to the Campus Police Substance Abuse Enforcement to try and lessen my fine for getting caught too drunk underaged. This letter was just one of many letters to the cops throughout the year... yikes.

To Whom It May Concern:

On the events of March 23rd, 2016, the police came to my room around 7:30pm. I had just recently returned to my room where I was sleeping when I was awoken to loud knocking on my door. I answered and followed all orders that the two police officers demanded. However, during these events, I felt extremely victimized. The officers went on to ask me confusing questions that did not relate to the situation, in efforts to intentionally confuse me. They then informed me that the Corbett front office was responsible for calling them to my room after I had asked for a key. I do not know why the staff at Corbett front desk would feel the need to call these officers to my room. This ticket is extremely unfair due to the fact that Corbett and staff reinforce the idea that we as students are encouraged to come back to Corbett, as it is our safe place. I did not disturb anyone or cause any mishap. I simply asked for a key, and returned to my room alone, where I went to bed. I also feel that this ticket is wrong because there is no tangible evidence that I was under the influence of alcohol. The officers never asked me to take a Breathalyzer test. I was safe in my room sleeping when the cops knocked, demanded I open the door, and started interrogating me. While Corbett is supposed to be my "safe place", I find myself feeling uncomfortable and unsafe when returning back now. I felt victimized because there was no reasoning behind why Corbett would find it necessary to call the cops. Innocently, with nothing to hide, I gave the two officers permission to search my room. The search of my room was unnecessary. Given that there was nothing to hide, the officers did not find anything. I was in my room, my personal space, where I should be entitled to the privacy I deserve. Due to my challenging major and heavy workload, I went to bed fairly early, so I could get adequate sleep for the busy week ahead of me. That being said, I am a good student, I was not breaking any law, and I am responsible. School is my number one priority, and this incident has caused me extra stress that is unneeded. Instead of focusing on school and grades, I am dealing with this ticket that was completely undeserved. I am writing today to appeal and revoke the ticket I was given. This incident was extremely unnecessary. I hope that in the efforts of staff here at Colorado State University, those in charge will take my explanation into consideration. I would be happy to discuss this issue with anybody necessary in order to claim my innocence and reverse this ticket. Thank you for your time.

Sincerely,
Elli Cikovic

Okay so, *apparently*, the cops were knocking at my door and I didn't answer for a while, but when I eventually did, I answered the door with just a blanket wrapped around me and couldn't speak properly. (This is what my hall-mates told me the next day that were watching.) Given, it was 2 p.m. (yikes), and I was blacked the fuck out, like do not remember anything. *Apparently*, I was trying to lie my way out of the whole thing and it was just *so* bad. Fuck, I wish I remember exactly what I said. I also still wonder what I said that made the front desk call the police on me. It was probably just because I was in zombie mode and they wanted to make sure I was alive — makes sense. Ugh, why did I always have to lose my keys when blacked out?! They definitely fined my ass.

Also, pretty sure Fiona helped me edit this letter. Lol.

Freshman Year Short & Sad Story

Towards the end of freshman year, I woke up one morning to a loud knocking at my door after a bad blackout. It was a 40-ish year-old brown-haired man in a black sweater that said he was campus police. However, he wasn't just any police — he said he was the campus assault police. Considering that I did not remember anything from the night other than being escorted to my dorm at like 3 a.m., I answered very confused. It's actually weird though because I do have like a third-party memory from being found... like I am out of my body looking down and I see myself lying on the floor of some random hallway and a few RA's hovered over me all worried. Anyways, the guy wanted to talk. He took me to the common area of my dorm, closed the door, and sat me down. He was being nice to me, maybe even too nice, so I knew I wasn't in trouble, which also confused me. He then started asking all kinds of unsettling questions like, "Do you remember what happened last night?" "Do you remember who you were with?" "Do you remember being found?" Well, no sir, the last thing I remember was being at the lacrosse party and then bam — blackout. *Apparently*, I was found passed out in the hallway of a dorm that was not mine and was honestly pretty far, and my clothing was for lack of better terms... not on correctly. Ugh, why was it always the lacrosse parties? So, yeah, he said I was most likely roofied and... you know... based on the state I was found. Nice. I asked the guy if I could go back to my room because I was crying so hysterically. I also asked him to stop asking questions and to never come back.

Guess when you're found post-rape like, they spare you an underage drinking ticket. Thank god because this one would have been my third, and the police told me during my previous hearing that another one could lead to expulsion. So, maybe it was a good thing?

(To answer that question, absolutely not. This was beyond horrific to face alone and I almost didn't even put this story in the book.)

21

Antidepressants and Binge Drinking

"Jesus loves me, this I know. For He gave me Lexapro." - Glennon Doyle

There's a difference between feeling "depressed" and having an actual chemical imbalance that needs treatment. I have a chemical imbalance. Probably a few to be honest. That's why I take antidepressants. Some people believe SSRI's make you "numb" but that is not the case, at least not for me. I am still able to feel all the highs and lows in life, *to extreme levels*, with my medicine. I am just able to assess my feelings now too, rather than going into an immediate full-blown manic episode. Or having OCD rule my life, which would probably be the case without my Lexapro. Sure, my mental health is still a daily challenge — but at least it's manageable now. And that is because of my pretty little antidepresso's and remaining *alcohol-free*.

Let me dive a little deeper. Medication helps me think logically rather than with an immediate emotional freak out. It puts me on a safe rollercoaster of emotions. Before medication, I was living on a drop tower, just waiting for my emotions to come, and then bam — drop — bam — crazy lady. Now, instead of living like that I now live on one of those newer speed coasters. The ones that go up and down, sometimes upside down, but smoothly and rarely to malfunction, at least not fatally. I prefer a little speed rather than a daily drop to my death. You feel?

I was first put on antidepressants at the age of sixteen. It was right around the time that the Twitter account was made. I was just not okay and my therapist knew I needed something. And since then, I have been on Zoloft, Wellbutrin, Prozac, and now Lexapro. I would get drunk a lot on the first three (bad idea), but Lexapro was the lucky winner in the end. Once I was put on it, things started to feel more normal. I quit drinking within my first year on it. Interesting to think about that while writing this out. I *love* Lexapro. But it took me time to find that right one, which is the biggest downside to these types of medications in my opinion. You pretty much have to try them all before you find the one that fits, and it can be a gruesome process.

I respect those who don't want to be on medication as I never wanted to be myself, but I am. At least for now. I tried to go off of them for a few months from late 2019 to early 2020 and let's just say my emotions were... unmanageable. Maybe one day I will be medication free when I am stupid rich and live on a yacht, but for now, I need them to survive in this matrix of a world that we live in.

I never felt the full benefits of my medication until I put down alcohol, which was also something my therapist(s) had been telling me to do for years. Turns out, I just love to play with fire, and that I did. Antidepressants made my blackouts worse. I lost even more control — I went even darker. My poor pills didn't stand a chance when I was binge drinking. I would often lose my Zoloft and Wellbutrin in college or just forget to take it half the time. College Elli was a mess, please don't judge her. And again, I need to mention that I am not a doctor or medical specialist. This is still my diary.

Drinking on antidepressants is a risk. Sure, I was still blacking out before getting on medication, but once I started taking it, my blackouts became even more "zombie like." Also, the medicine absolutely affected my weight. I gained 25 pounds in three months my senior year of high school. It was hard. I just had no control over my body... for so long... in so many ways. This was also at the same time when I was having issues with not being able to shit for weeks at a time. God that was such a dark and... dense time for my body. I wish I could give that version of me a hug. Well, I am — by writing this.

If you are on medication, I really hope you don't also binge drink daily. It's not good for you. You are doing more damage than good, take it from an expert.

It's also so interesting now to learn that not all people with alcoholism (AUD) "blackout" while using. I swear I thought you had to blackout in order to be an alcoholic. Every alcoholic in my family does, so I just thought it was normal. Like I could not imagine remembering all the cringy shit I did, but I guess some people do. That might be even worse. I was always a "lights out, no one is home" drunk, probably mostly due to abusing alcohol on powerful medication.

I was sitting with some girlfriends at the end of 2023 and they were talking about the *maybe* 1-2 times they blacked out in their life and don't remember anything. I was just sitting there thinking in my head, "Shit, there's about five months straight that I don't remember from 2018 when I was living in Prague." Europe was a blackout. And I think I lost my medication for a few weeks while out there. Not good.

So much alcohol consumed with no recollection. What a waste. What was I feeding? Some monster, I swear. The **alcoholic monster**. An endless pitted beast ready to feed off of my guilt and inner shame. Ready to embarrass me to the point of tarnishing almost all of my relationships. What a little fucker. Got you now. No more monster here.

"I will drown you in sorrow and ruin your life!"

Since I was fourteen, every single one of my doctors, including therapists(s) and psychiatrist(s), told me that I should not drink. Especially once they put me on medication. Every single one of them said it, for years. And then during every single appointment after, I would be sitting in their office crying about some shit I did blacked out. I just never thought I could quit, that was a death sentence to me then.

I would also freak out any time a doctor put me on a steroid or heavy medication that said, "do not drink with medication." The thought of not being able to drink for a week or more was worse than death. I would ask them all types of manipulative questions like, "Well what would happen if I just drank for two days while on it?" or "Well what would really happen to my liver if I just had like one to two drinks a day?" And still, every time they said not to do it. And every time, I still did. Which usually resulted in an even more demon like possessed blackout.

It took me ten years to listen. I remember I even fucking cried once at the doctors when they put me on a serious antibiotic and said I absolutely could not drink for two weeks. Like how could I ever go two weeks without drinking? I don't think I even ended up taking the medication that time. My addiction ran deep.

But still, without knowing, all of these doctor's voices were planted deep into my subconscious mind and I do believe that their voices helped me quit. They just needed to compound... a lot.

So, I hope I can be that voice to you. You do not need alcohol to be happy, it is actually (probably) the one thing blocking you from it. And please, listen to the doctors when they tell you not to drink. I probably have some permanent brain damage or some shit.

22

Family Fights (Short Story)

The summer before going back to college for my sophomore year, my family and I were invited to friend group pool party. Really, it's just a group of my parents' friends and their families that I have known since I was a baby who have all partied together for years. There were around twenty of us set to attend on this particular day.

My dad, mom, and stepmom were all going, which is common for my family, and luckily for me there were some college aged kids going to be there as well. We all come from parents who love to drink, so obviously the apples do not fall far from the trees. Us "kids" all decided to steal some of the alcohol and get hammered. I drank so many rum and cokes that I lost count.

Me and one guy in particular took it *very* far.

We blacked out so hard that, *apparently*, his mom found us making out in a back room, which neither of us remember. He also had a girlfriend at the time, so icing on the cake. *Fuck me.*

When I came out of my blackout a few hours later, still at the party (post make-out), I was in the middle of a screaming fight with my dad and stepmom. Like the worst one ever. And I don't even remember how it started.

My mom was sitting with me trying to defend me, and some of the guys my age jumped in, but honestly, we were all hammered and I still don't even know what we were fighting about.

I just knew it was a fucking mess and I was crying — a lot.

Once the fight simmered down, my dad somehow got us all home. He was pissed. My flight was early the next morning to go back to Colorado and he was telling me that I wasn't going back. I think I ran away and threw up when he said that. I was still so drunk.

Somehow, I ended up convincing him that I would be okay and needed to get back to school for my education, lol. Everything is truthfully pretty blurry from this memory and it is one that I have definitely tried to suppress. I had just spent the entire summer sneaking to old high school "friends" parties and having sad blackouts, so I wasn't in a good head space by any means. I was also trying to lose my freshman fifteen (forty), which was depressing in itself. Only now do I see that the real weight I needed to lose was not physical. That summer was one of the worst.

Luckily, I made it on my flight to go back to Colorado, but I wasn't okay. And the only solution I had was to blackout some more. Our past follows us, we can't just run from it. Especially not with a bottle.

That day party was the last time I saw and spoke to my family before a *monstrous* drinking year. I didn't know what to do with my feelings other than to drown them. My drinking just kept getting worse. Alcoholism is such a brutal disease.

23

The Adventures of Elli and Macy

I met another one of my favorite people in the world my sophomore year of college. We were set to be "random roommates" since we both had a mutual friend that needed two extras in the apartment we wanted — but nothing was *random* about Macy and I living together. Our first encounter was by accident, a few days prior to our move in, at the local country bar. This was just a few days after the massive fight I had with my family

I was blacked out (of course) and, *apparently*, we saw each other on the dance floor and screamed something like, "Holy shit are we going to be best friends?!?" and by the next morning, we were family. I say this because I actually ended up making out with her brother on the dance floor, something I do not fully recall, and then when I woke up the next morning on some random basement floor, I first saw her brother next to me, and I was like fuck, not again. But then I turned over the other way and I saw Macy lying next to me too. Turns out this basement floor was just twenty minutes outside of campus and belonged to Macy's family and we all passed out on it after the drunken night. You would think that I would have been more scared or uncomfortable, but with Macy next to me, I immediately felt the opposite. Macy is unlike any woman you will ever meet. She is a one-of-a-kind magical human being. We are blessed to have her walking this earth. She is a true *wild woman*. And so, I found myself again with someone that I could be my true authentic self. All walls were down with Macy. And I knew immediately that she was going to be my new best friend.

Macy didn't judge me; she doesn't judge anyone. She made me feel loved, seen, and heard. She was also a D1 athlete running the heptathlon for CSU, which is like totally insane. A true athletic beast and I swear she didn't even have to try. However, I quickly learned that her true talents were off of the track field.

Our rooms ended up being right next to each other in our new apartment, which was perfect. We were living at The District, aka the party apartments, and were on the first floor with our balcony right on the pool deck, so our backyard was about to be consistent pool fucking parties. A very wild year of party throwing was ahead of us. Athlete parties. Our mutual friend that we lived with was on the Swim & Dive team and she loved those damn football players, so we threw some of the biggest athlete parties of the year.

When Macy and I partied, we partied hard. Our energies brought out the craziest, most fun, and most *dangerous* sides of each other. She was the missing piece of my soul, and I needed her. We are cut from the same cloth. Also, going from a depressing summer in Pittsburgh living with my dad to a party apartment living with Macy was... incredible. I was free. I was happy. Well, as happy as a secretly depressed alcoholic can be.

But still, it is safe to say that two stars were born that year. *Party stars.* Macy also had access to American Airlines companion passes, which is why we were able to travel so much. There is no way that Macy and I could afford to do the things we did without many slight finesses, one being the passes. We always knew how to ball on a budget — or at least tried.

We kept a journal titled *The Adventures of Elli and Macy*, hence the title for this chapter, with stories written out in a drunken manor — but they are too chaotic to put into this book. So instead, I want to share my favorite story about the time we went to her family friend's, aka Rich Man Ray's, mansion in Scottsdale, Arizona. We flew down over break via the companion passes, and after a few days of aggressive partying in the mansion with Macy's family and like fifteen other people I just met, we decided it was a good idea to take Rich Man Ray's Chevy Tahoe down across the Mexican border... in the middle of the night. If my dad ever reads this (hopefully not), I am so sorry, because I totally lied about this trip. No one in my family knew that I went to Mexico, let alone almost got kidnapped by the Mexican police cartel. Yikes. Okay, here we go.

Mexico With Macy

Picture this — three hot blonde 20-year-olds driving a 2000 Chevy Tahoe through the Arizona desert with nothing but the Eagles Greatest Hits album blasting. We were driving to Puerto Penasco, Mexico. Macy and me in the front, and our other friend, X, in the back seat.

We were driving in Rich Man Rays' Chevy Tahoe. Rich Man Ray is not a sugar daddy, but he is close. He owns a beautiful house, one of many, in a gated community outside of Scottsdale, Arizona. Think massive, open back, infinity pool, private driveway, 10+ bedrooms, and movie theatre kind of house. When I first went there, things changed for me. I learned that you don't need a shit ton of money to have a baller ass time, you just need to know someone that does! That is what Macy and her family taught me. We had a party mansion, for free. And we were always invited, just needed to make sure we could get on the American Airlines standby list.

This specific trip was during Thanksgiving Break 2017. After a few days of partying with Macy's family and their friends, they all had to go back to their normal lives, but Macy and I had a few more days off from school. Ray's house was not far from the Mexican border and I had never been able to drink legally, so we had the bright idea to drive to Mexico for *dem legal margz*, of course! We asked Ray if we could borrow one of his cars and *of course* he immediately handed over the keys to a Tahoe that had been sitting in the garage for years.

We were on our way. We were cruising. Eagles blasting. No problems in sight... other than getting across the Mexican border with an obscene amount of underage alcohol. Once we got close, it started to get dark, and to our luck, the back window of the car broke. Like the window was wide open and would not close. And we were driving through some of those neighborhoods on the border where your window **should** be up... and tinted. We finally made it to the border patrol and that's when they started to search our car. We were nervous. We had bottles of Kirkland Vodka, Captain Morgan, Malibu, and Fireball in the back wrapped up in sweatshirts in the blue suitcase. They started checking the back and Macy was SWEATING, like so much. So clammy. But to our luck they searched every bag except the blue one that carried the bottles. Macy is a good luck charm, I swear.

So, after we made it through the border, we were off to find our hotel... that didn't exist. We had no idea where we were going. We didn't have a proper hotel booked. *But* what we did know was that there were bars that would accept our IDs. So fuck it, we would find somewhere to stay!

Quick Note: Before leaving, Macy's mom told us about a woman that was kidnapped and scalped by the cartel when crossing the border. Why did we not let this concern us? Good question. We just wanted to party. Plus, karma always seemed to be on our side. We were good people, good girls, just looking for a good time.

On the way to try and find a hotel, we stopped at a Mexican Tree Farm (yes, I am telling the truth) to try and get the window fixed. It was midnight and no one spoke a lick of English, but turns out our friend in the backseat spoke fluent Spanish. Just our luck! So, with a little help from the friendly locals, we eventually got our window fixed, found a hotel, and got settled in. We were bummed to realize that the entire area was dead, other than the locals, but we still got ready to go and find a local bar to hit full send. And like usual, we got fucking plastered.

Once we got to the Tekila Bar, yes it was called the Tekila Bar, we made some friends. A random Texas couple was there and then some locals. The bartender became our new best friend and he gave me some sort of shot that is illegal in the US, and after I took it, I immediately ran to the bathroom to throw up. He called it the "worm" shot, and yes, there was a worm in it, so of course I threw up, and then of course came back to rally. I was a pro at the "puke and rally." At one point I remember taking over the DJ booth at the bar, and then a blurry car ride home to our hotel in a... Hummer. Not the Tahoe.

When we woke up, we were so sick, but alive and in one piece. Except Macy had lost her phone... again. This girl lost her phone more than anyone I have ever known, including myself, which was hard to beat. *Apparently*, we went swimming in the hotel pool when we came back from the bar and there were guys who said they were "pool boys" hanging out too. We are pretty sure the "pool boys" took the phone because it was 2 a.m. and this was not the kind of hotel (motel) that had *pool boys*. Macy's phone was done for.

Then we had another morning surprise because we realized we had gotten too drunk and took a free ride home in the Texas couple's Hummer, which meant we left our car at the bar... miles away. Y'all, there are no Ubers let alone taxis in this small town *and* it was Thanksgiving. So, Macy and I volunteered to go get the car — by foot, at 8 a.m. I don't want to be in-polite, but the area that we were in was... fucking *sketch*. And we were hungover as fuck. However, to our advantage, when you are that hungover you just don't care as much about your surroundings. Also both of our stomachs *hurt*. The housekeeper had warned us about Montezuma's revenge the day before, but we had too many endorphins to deal that just yet. We had to try and find the missing car. And phone.

Macy and I got started on our journey and I swear not even five minutes into walking the streets, a Mexican Police Car pulled up right next to us. We were horrified, because... cartel. But that's not actually how this story goes.

Hector. I will never forget Hector. He was a heavyset, loud man in a *little* police outfit driving the car. His "partner" was a quiet female officer. Hector immediately fancied Macy, most men do, and offered to give us a ride. We knew that we shouldn't get into the random police car because it was *sketchy*, but fuck it, we were sick and had no idea where this bar was, and Hector said he knew. So we got in and the four of us were sitting side by side in a SINGLE ROW police mobile. No backseat. Bench style. Hector's female partner looked petrified and did not speak a lick of English. My stomach started to hurt even more.

If I was with anyone else, I would have never gotten in that vehicle. But with Macy, things were different. We were each other's "devil on the shoulder." We looked at each other at the same time, said fuck it, and jumped in. Hector was friendly... a little too friendly. And then it happened. He started KISSING

Macy. I'm not making this up. Like singing to and KISSING her. Me and the lady cop looked at each other like "Whaaaaaat!" and Hector continued to sing and dance right in Macy's face saying things like, "Call me Hector," "Say my name," "Kiss me!" Okay, by this point, from an outsider's perspective, you would think it's a wrap. He was going to take us, scalp us, and sell us for parts — all while making out with Macy. But no, that never happened. Macy was too pure. He couldn't hurt her. And he eventually dropped us right off at the Chevy Tahoe.

I still don't understand how all of this panned out, but things always did for us. We called this memory "cartel kisses" in our journal. Cartel kisses from Hector. It was really funny then, but looking back at it now, we really could have died. Again, sorry if you are reading this dad.

Once we got back into the car we booked it to the hotel, because once the endorphins fell off, Montezuma's revenge kicked in. I took the toilet, Macy on the sink, and X in the bathtub. Both ends. Think the movie *Bridesmaids*, that's literally what was going on in that bathroom. But then, magically out of nowhere, the same housekeeper knocked on the door and offered us some magic pills to help with the attack of the Montezuma. And after about 30 minutes, the constant diarrhea and vomiting went away. I still wonder to this day what that pill was, had to be *magic.*

We were scheduled to stay at the hotel for two more days, but after the missing phone, missing car, and multiple close encounters with death, we decided to hit the beach one more time, say goodbye, and take it back to the Arizona mansion. We figured ordering Chinese and watching movies in Rich Man Ray's theatre was a better idea. And it sure the fuck was.

This was just an average week for us. I lived out 100 year's worth of life in that one year living with Macy. We have countless stories, but I don't have time for them in this book. Maybe I will tell the story about when we went to the X-Games in Aspen and stayed at a friend's ski house, but couldn't afford food, so we lived off of Burnetts and Adderall for a week. That one ended a little tragically though, so I will probably save it for a later date.

I miss living with Macy. Life has ups and downs and some major life changes occurred, but Macy is still one of my best friends today. I am who I am because of her. I am who I am because of all the amazing women in my life. But 2017-2018 really was extra special because of her.

I was on Facetime with Macy while finishing this book in April of 2024 and she looked at me and said, "Elli, if anyone can do it all, it's you. You can do it all." I needed to hear that. She always had a way of motivating me. It was just that morning that I was looking in the mirror and doubting myself, and this book. But hearing those words out of her mouth just hit me different, they always do.

Macy, I love you more than you will ever know and I will always want to see you do a back flip at a frat party.

P.S. You were always too cool for school.

24

Spring Breaker

They say, "What happens on spring break, stays on spring break." But for me, it was more like, "What happened should never have happened because what the *actual fuck*, Elli."

Over my four years in college, I took a few "spring break" trips. These trips contain some of the worst blacking out of my life and the most IDGAF moments I can recount. I remember getting back to campus and feeling dead inside for at least a month following each of these trips. It went as far as me being put on Fox News's *Hannity*... a classic video that I still have in my possession.

I decided to summarize all four trips to give a basic outlook on how drastic they were but have also decided not to share everything. Some details just aren't necessary for the plot of this book.

Lake Havasu — 2016

A group of my girlfriends and I planned a trip to Lake Havasu, Arizona for our freshman year spring break trip. Our plan was to fly into Vegas, take an Uber to Lake Havasu for a few days, and then Uber back to Vegas for a night or two to stay at the Stratosphere. The Uber to Lake Havasu was about three hours. Not sure whose bright idea that was, but shit, we made it work. Lake Havasu was known to be a massive spring break riot. It's a "party on the lake" with thousands of college students from all over the county. We didn't care how we got there, we just needed to make it in one piece. The number of times in college that I spent an obnoxious amount of money on Ubers was uncalled for. For this specific ride there were six girls — three of us in the back seat, and the other three of us in the truck bed of some random guy's pickup who said yes to drive us that far. We even convinced this guy to stop at In-N-Out because we had never been and then Walmart, of course, to buy us a couple handles of vodka for the week. Kinda creepy to think back on how he bought all of us 19-year-old girls handles of liquor and drove us over three hours across multiple state borders. But back then, he was just a *nice guy*.

This trip was a blur. Our first day there, we met a group of sugar daddies and spent the day doing drugs on their yacht. It was beautiful from what I can remember, however, at this time I was in the depth of my depression and about 30 pounds overweight. So, I wasn't feeling good in a bikini. But hey, as long as I had a handle of vodka and some cocaine, I could figure out how to have a good time, aka *blackout*. I just remember always feeling disgusting and uncomfortable in my own skin, so I would compensate that with drinking more. This is just one example of a time where I was doing pretty cool shit, but all I could think about was my shame and disgust in my own skin, therefore needing to blackout to get out of it. And therefore, not remembering multiple amazing experiences. We went cliff diving that day and I don't remember it, but I do have a video of myself jumping which is cool. The boat really was stunning. And the sugar daddies were sugarin'.

There are a few key moments from this trip I feel like I should share. One night I blacked out and "came to" on top of some guy on a Bud Light branded boat trying to fit his penis in me. It was so big. Massive. It just wouldn't fit. I think the pain of trying to fit it in is what took me out of my blackout. I didn't even know his name, still don't, but fuck did it hurt. Talk about reaching just to feel something. I was so numb inside back then. At least he was super hot. That same night I had my fake ID taken at some club, which had me in the need to get extra pissed drunk, considering I went through all that work to send $300 to some random man in China for it. Ugh.

A few nights later, my one friend and I met a group of football players. We ended up drinking with them and I blacked out, per usual. When I woke up, I was in bed with three guys, none of my girlfriends in sight. The wild part about this situation is that when I woke up and saw where I was, I was just like *oops*, another normal morning — just an entire team of large men and lil ole' me. I somehow found all of my belongings and ran back to my room to tell my friends about what happened. Their response was something like, "Oh just Elli being Elli!" As if it was a normal situation. Like I might have literally had sex with multiple men and have no recollection. *Apparently*, my friend was begging me to leave with her but I wouldn't listen. Gosh I was so stubborn — sometimes just downright mean too. Now, I understand that these consistent behaviors are absolutely not normal. It was just what I did, for years. I didn't know any better.

I always adventured alone, searching for something in the pits of my blackouts, not really sure what. I think I was always looking for love and protection. Little did I know, I was searching in all the wrong places. My blackouts always left me in extreme and sometimes dangerous situations with *no* love and definitely *no* protection. These behaviors were consistent. Safe to say the rest of the trip was a blur, but I survived. *Always.*

South Padre — 2017

South Padre, TX was some of the craziest partying and blacking out I have ever done. I almost died that week, multiple times. This trip is also the one where I was featured on Fox News's *Hannity* in a segment regarding, "College Spring Breakers spending all their parent's money to binge drink and cause destruction, death pools are rising." So ya, it wasn't good.

The aftermath of this trip on my health, mental and physical, still scares me to this day. It was just bad. So bad. Girl gone wild x10, and I'm pretty sure I traumatized some of the girls that I went with.

Apparently, a lot of sex trafficking has happened in South Padre, which means I probably should have been concerned about that considering how much I was drinking. Also, there were zero Ubers down there. It felt like a different world. A more dangerous world. I had countless blackouts consisting of waking up in different hotels with different guys. I don't even know how many people I actually slept with that week. These are not moments that I am proud of. And I hated myself for it.

At one point during the trip, around ten of us piled on the back of some random guy's golf cart trying to make it to the Migos concert. We were going at least 35 MPH on this thing and my drunk ass decided to take a sip of my drink off the back and nearly flew off. I swear I was .05 seconds away from plunging to my death. I think three people died that weekend. And the Migos never even showed up. What a waste. All I wanted was to hear "T-Shirt" live.

Burnetts. Every morning. Wake up and take shots. No breakfast. Just shots. That's how all-day partying mornings start where I'm from. Blacked out by noon.

I will give one specific example from the trip that still haunts me to this day. The last night we went out partying, knowing damn well we had to catch a 6 a.m. shuttle to catch to the airport, and I "decided" to blackout and leave my friends. When I came out of my blackout, I was walking onto an airport shuttle bus outside of a random hotel half dressed. *Apparently*, I got so drunk and ran away from my friends with some random guy. One of the girls, my saving angel, packed all my shit, which was a mess, tracked my phone, and somehow found me in one of the hundreds of rooms at 5:30 a.m. Like holy fuck, talk about a good person, and she somehow convinced the shuttle driver to go to my tracked location. *Apparently*, the guy I was with brought me down and made out with me in front of the entire shuttle of random people. And again, it was 6 a.m. and I was in booty shorts still drunk as fuck, no underwear, just reeking of cheap booze and sweaty sex. I have zero recollection of meeting that guy or how I got to his hotel. I have zero recollection of having sex with him. And I also have zero recollection of getting to the shuttle. But once I stepped on and felt the cold breeze through my vagina showing shorts, I *came to*. Gosh, the thought of doing something like that today horrifies me. I get a panic attack if I am late to a doctor's appointment now so I couldn't imagine doing the shit my 20-year-old self was. My friend there saved me. I would have been fucked if I woke up in that guy's bed with my friends halfway back to Colorado. Thank you, Kaylee, if you are reading this. A true savior.

Okay, before I continue the story, I have to mention that that same guy ended up shipping my underwear (and purse which I apparently left) to my apartment in box. I guess it was romantic, they were folded and everything. He also ended up flying all the way to Denver to see me, but I ended up never meeting him at the airport. I told myself that I was an asshole for doing that back then, but the truth is that I was terrified of him considering I didn't remember anything from our night together. Another guy from South Padre also drove to my college town to hang out with me and came to my apartment. It was awkward, because again, I didn't really remember him, and we had the most awkward sex that night. I googled him after he left and found out he got kicked off of his football team for credit card fraud, so that's nice. He had also, *apparently*, just gotten out of jail — also nice. After blackout sex sometimes I thought that if I slept with them sober(ish) it would mean that I was *in control* those nights and that I *wanted* to do those things. Turns out that wasn't so true most of the time. Sex is such a deep connection, and to do it and not remember... well... it is a unique feeling. Not in a good way.

Okay so back to the original story and getting to the airport. I was a disaster and had lost my ID during my *adventurous* night. And I don't really remember how I pulled this one off, but I somehow managed to use a picture of my ID that I had on my phone to get on my flight. Master class level convincing, I guess. I truly don't know how I pulled off most of the shit I did back then.

The story gets worse. When we were waiting for our flight in the terminal, I was woken up aggressively by a clerk because, *apparently*, I was laying down on the floor and my VAGINA was hanging out of my booty shorts. Could you imagine seeing a girl passed out on the floor of the airport and her vagina flaps are hanging out? Like that is fucked up. And that's not it y'all. I threw up IN MY HANDS on the airplane. The flight attendant threatened to do an emergency landing because of it, but I begged her in the back not to. She thankfully had a heart because I would have been fucked, like definitely arrested upon landing, my BAC was probably ridiculous. And the condition I was in...yikes. Oh, and no ID.

I am blessed to have had friends that put up with all this bullshit and helped me survive. I would be dead without them. I think everyone knew that I had a problem, because when I was sober, I was great. But Drunk Elli... she was so... difficult. She was different, not in a good way. I have one word for this trip. *Shame.*

Macy, whom I was living with at the time back on campus, recently told me she never went on a spring break because of my stories from this trip. I don't blame her.

Berlin & Amsterdam — 2018

While I was studying abroad in Prague, a few friends from school flew in for spring break and we spent two days in Berlin followed by three days in Amsterdam. Our hostel in Amsterdam was booked for Saint Patrick's Day weekend, which was a *wild* time to be there. My male friend, X, was a part of the group that visited. He was also a blackout artist and we have had some crazy adventures together.

Berlin was a blackout. I did some questionable things, per usual. But the culture was great. And we did get to see some historical locations, which I am grateful for. I hooked up with one of the guys in our friend group on the bathroom floor of the hostel, drunk as shit. He is actually a nice guy, so not totally mad about that, but again, why did I always have to fuck someone?

Then came Amsterdam. The night of the bar crawl. Well, I don't remember much of that night. I don't even remember starting the crawl itself. It was a crazy day. What I do remember though is that the guy I had been seeing on and off again in Prague showed up at the bar in AMSTERDAM?! Like come on, how did he end up there? He always brought out an ugly side of me. All boys who wouldn't love me back did. Ugh. But I will get to more on him later.

The hostel that we stayed in was above an Irish Pub, go figure. *Side note:* Amsterdam is an amazing city, and I am honestly happy that I got to experience it while still drinking, but I definitely need to go back while sober. I don't remember half this trip. But I do know that it was an inspirational city.

Back to the bar crawl — I don't even remember starting the damn bar crawl, I blacked out way before it even started. But *apparently,* I drank my way through the entire thing. At one point I remember coming out of my blackout and my phone was gone. Losing your phone in Europe is not okay, I was freaking out while going in and out of the darkness. Turns out my friend, X, had it the whole time. We were sharing my phone... and credit card at this point. Poor X got robbed on the train in Berlin. So, there we were, two blackout artists sharing a phone and credit card. That was a dangerous game, but we survived. *Always.*

This night is one that I really wish I remembered. Like how could I not remember ten different bars that we went to? An entire night in one of the coolest cities in the world, and I have nothing to recall from it. Like, that fucking sucks. Alcohol fucking sucks. However, later on, after the bar crawl, there was finally a moment that snapped me out of my blackout. And that was... *The Red-Light District.* X and I had left the group because he wanted to show me some of the crazy shit that the leader of the pub crawl, think crazy young Irish man mixed with Van Wilder, had shown him. And this is when we entered the sex show area of Amsterdam. I sort of remember going to a couple of the shows, but one moment in particular took me completely out of my blackout and back into the present moment. And that was... X and I standing in one of the Red-Light prostitute's private rooms off the main drag and her yelling, "200 Euro for a threesome!" at us. I remember *coming to* at this exact moment and just looking around the room — it was sort of shocking. I mean first there was the naked Russian chick yelling at us, but it was also just the room itself. I remember a lot of purple and then red flashing lights. The bed had dark sheets and there was a small trashcan full of condoms in the corner. X was just as drunk as me so he was staring at me like "What the fuck do we do?!" I looked at the prostitute and then I looked back at X and I said, "RUN!" We went for the exit, but just as we were getting there this massive lady pimp came out from the back hallway and was yelling at us in an even deeper, scarier Russian accent, "You must pay, you must pay!" Thankfully, we escaped onto the street. I think X still has a video of her yelling at us. *Classic.*

Now, I understand that we were just drunk idiots who were disrupting business, so her yelling was valid, but fuck no were we paying $200 for a three-some. I was broke. And that room was scary. Also, X and I were never like that, he's a brother to me. We did however go to one of the shows where you put in 1 euro and go into a little room with cum all over the floor and got to watch two people fucking on a spinning bed. That was pretty neat. But really, Europe was just one big blackout. I grew a lot while there, sure, but I was also drinking every single day. Drinking away my sadness, as always. I had some serious family and friendship hardships going on in America while I was in Europe, which led me to drink even more. *Always.*

Oh yeah, the day after the Red-Light blackout, we took some shrooms to go to the butterfly observatory café. Gosh I was so excited for it, but the shrooms on top of a massive blackout hangover made me so sick, like couldn't walk straight sick. And sadly, I threw up in the butterfly cafe. The butterflies were so beautiful, and I couldn't even enjoy them, because of fucking alcohol. If you know me, you know I love butterflies. I have a massive tattoo of one on my left shoulder. But I was too sick to love them that day, and I swear I threw up black tar in that bathroom — think it might have been the devil.

Laguna Beach — 2019

My senior year I went to Laguna Beach to one of my best friends, Hannah's, house. I thought this was going to be a really chill spring break, just me Hannah and one of my other best friends, Ida. But then we ran into some of the CSU football players on the beach and they invited us to a pool party the next day. This guy had a mansion, like cheetah print carpet mansion in Laguna Beach. My dream house. But of course, I blacked out thirty minutes into the party. Why did I always have to pregame with double shots? Ugh. I don't remember anything after sitting in his beautiful back yard for like one drink. *Apparently,* we went to a restaurant, a whole other house, and a karaoke bar. Like eight hours of activities and I remember absolutely none of it. This was one of the most disappointing blackouts for me because I thought I was happy at this time. I had an amazing boyfriend ready to move wherever I did after graduation, I was set to graduate business school with a high GPA, and I was with two of my best friends in beautiful Laguna fucking Beach for five days. But no, on day two, I had to blackout... bad. Liquor was always in control. I thought I would be able to handle it while in a happier position in my life, but that was false.

There's a video of me sitting at the pool party earlier in the day and I'm just like bobbing in and out, staring at nothing, so blacked out. I was so embarrassed when I woke up and found out how much I had "missed." I also had a few missed calls from my boyfriend, which was fair considering my texts to him made no fucking sense. He was concerned, fairly. But he was a trooper. Ugh, it was supposed to be a relaxing trip, no blackouts, one last "hurrah" with my besties before adulthood. But instead, I was lying in bed all day trying to figure out why I fucking hated myself so much to keep living like that. My poor friends never knew what to do with me on days like that, I was always so depressed after an unwanted blackout. I was so mad at myself because it was such a great trip... until it wasn't.

It makes me sad to look back and wonder what I looked like to people that didn't know me in public. They probably felt bad for me, like how I feel bad for people that I see too drunk out now. I was a lifeless zombie wandering around for hours at a time. Fuck, I am so grateful to be on the other side of all of this. And to have such amazing friends that always made sure I stayed alive.

Spring Break: 4
Elli: 0

25

PRAGUE

I am honestly in awe that I survived living in Europe for six months as a legal drinker. I went out and drank almost every single night, and most days too, in various countries. The cities that I visited, and blacked out in, are as follows: Prague (where I lived), Barcelona, Berlin, Amsterdam, Brussels, Munich, Split, Salzburg, and Vienna. Obviously, I cannot dive into every story because that would be a book in and of itself, but let me tell you at least a little bit about my time overseas.

I arrived in Prague on January 24th, 2018, when I was twenty years old. A few of my friends from school were enrolled in the same program and we had two weeks before our classes started at the University of Central and Eastern European Studies, which is an international business school located in Prague (Praha 3). The school was beautiful, the city was even more so, and the drinks were *pouring*. The night scene was unlike anything I had experienced before. A semester of partying, with no potential underage charges, was right at my fingertips.

But of course, a boy that was ready to break my heart had to step right into the picture. I met X during the Valentine's Day Party, which I do not remember, hosted by our school at a club the day before classes started. I woke up the morning after, confused per usual, and I was not in my tiny dorm bed, and I did not see my sweet, kind, and beautiful roommate (God bless you Lauren) lying across from me. No, I was in a stranger's bed, miles away. I was in X's bed. And my phone had no service, so I was extra lost and confused. This, however, was one of the rare occasions that when I looked over to see who I hooked up with during a blackout, I did not internally scream. He was hot. And *cool*. And this love affair lasted my entire stay in Europe. Okay, this "love affair" was really just me being obsessed over whoever, X in this case, gave me attention first, even though he showed absolutely zero signs of wanting anything more from me other than sex. But still, I was in love! Lord help me.

So yes, X had my heart for all of Europe. He would ignore me in class but once we ran into each other drunk at the club, instant love. Ugh. Don't worry though, I still slept with plenty of other guys and even hooked up with some of X's friends... in front of him. BUT, I was only doing all of that to get his attention so he would love me back! Haha, you see? Another semester of doing dumb shit drunk to try and get the attention of yet another unavailable asshole boy. I was so naïve, especially at twenty. I think I still am. I just have always wanted love. I am *such* a yearner, always fucking yearning.

Okay, so Europe was definitely a blur of blacking out, but I also had some deep self-discovery while living there. I left Europe a woman, a 21-year-old woman. I learned to accept myself more — the culture shock having a large part to do with that. Living outside of America for an extended period of time is something every US citizen should have to do. I understand that I am extremely fortunate to have done so, but to be honest, that semester was basically "free" because of my scholarship, student loans covering 4x tuition, and how damn cheap it is to live in Prague. But still, I know that it is not possible for everyone. However, I do think people find excuses not to travel. Just saying.

Another massive milestone occurred in my life while in Europe and that is: I discovered Lena Dunham and her book *Not That Kind of Girl* while traveling solo to Vienna. And if you know me, you know that book changed my damn life.

Amazing lifelong relationships were also formed during this time, but I also made a mess of myself. I pissed off people that I cared about and am fairly sure

I traumatized my poor roommate, Lauren. Lauren — if you are reading this, thank you for putting up with me being a blackout mess and sometimes raging bitch when hungover. You seriously are one of the most amazing people I know.

Okay time for some stories.

Absinthe. Absinthe is honestly something that I am grateful I was able to try before sobriety. Real absinthe, like secret bar behind the bar type of Absinthe. That shit took me to a different level. I loved taking those lime green devil shots in massive dance clubs and going all night. Good fucking times. But during all those "good times," nasty horrible hangovers followed where I would wake up and look at myself in the mirror, not knowing who the fuck was staring back at me. I was always lookihg in the mirror wondering who I *was* while living in Europe. But it's interesting because those six months were also a time where I started to not hate myself fully. I think it was the experience of new cultures, to be honest. It humbles you. However, I still hated how I *looked* in the mirror.

There was one night of blacking out about halfway through the semester when I "came to" and there was this beautiful French girl sitting next to me and yelling (kindly) in my face, "ARE YOU OKAY?!" I was not okay, clearly, and she ended up taking me home in a taxi that night. She was not the first random foreign person (angel) that got me home to my funky little dorm that semester. Not even close.

Okay, so school. Those classes... a fucking breeze. Especially for being one of the "top economic schools" in the world. Why? Well, lucky for us, the program did not reflect grades on our GPA, but only pass or fail. And to pass, you needed a 61%. Cake fucking walk. Especially for a sneaky little cheater like me. And I mean, come on, there was a BAR. Right in the middle of campus. They would make you a "martini" for 1 US dollar and said "martini" was really just a cup full of vodka. So, I drank a lot of vodka and watched a lot of European Netflix during those few months in class. Always hungover or drunk, of course.

Barcelona. I went to Barcelona one of my first weekends with two of my girlfriends. Barcelona was great, but I blacked out so hard in the club one night and left my friends to wander to the beach alone. I then, don't fully remember how this happened, ended up taking a horse and carriage with this random Spanish man back to our Airbnb and we fucked on the couch. I bet everyone heard us, as the Airbnb we had was not only shared with my two friends, but also a FAMILY OF STRANGERS. That was SO naughty of me! I don't even remember his name. Fuck, why did I always need an escape? Why did I need to prove my worth through sex? Sex that I would never remember. Why!

I went to SpringFest in Munich, wore the dirndl and everything. It was fun, but I was so insecure about the weight I had put on over the months in Europe, so of course, I over drank to try and get more "comfortable" in my skin. I remember dancing on the tables with beers and my friends, but then I browned out (close to a blackout, usually for an extended period of time), and "came to" while some random guy was going down on me in the woods, and then... on the Ferris wheel? I swear I time traveled some of those days between blackouts. Also, wow, I have no idea what he looked like or what his name was. I think he was German? Fuck.

One of my last days in Prague, a close girlfriend and I decided to bar hop around the castle and yes you guessed it — blackout. *Apparently*, after about bar #5, our drunk asses decided it was a good idea to do a photoshoot of me climbing up one of the ladders that hung off the side of the river wall. And just as you are expecting, I fell into the damn river. This river was fast, and it also morphed into a giant dam that would eat up anything on its path. *However*, somehow, someway, my lucky little self turned on my blackout superpowers and grabbed onto the next ladder before the drop and I escaped the current. Gosh... I get the shakes just thinking about this moment. This was absolutely one of those circumstances that wakes you up out of your blackout. I am still so grateful that I wasn't the bitch on the news the next day with a headline that stated, "International college student gets so drunk that she falls into the Vltava

River and dies." I still have the pictures from that day. I looked happy before the fall. Also, walking back to the tram and then dorms in a soaking wet outfit was a walk of shame I never expected to have that trip. *Thank. Fucking. God. For. My. Angels.*

Okay, before I wrap up my tales of Europe, I actually met a really cool guy and we danced all night at the clubs and ended up *making love* on the Charles Bridge — which was very bold if I must say so myself. That was a good night. I think we almost got caught and ended up moving behind some random car by the castle. Ugh, I miss seeing castles everyday.

Maybe I had just as many amazing experiences as bad ones while over there. And to be clear, the bad ones only ever happened during blackouts. Go figure. At least I came home alive.

That's it for now, goodbye.

26

Love & Alcohol

For so long all I ever seemed to care about were boys and alcohol... a deadly combination.

Ever since I was a little girl, I have believed in love. I just always felt that Prince Charming was going to come and save me one day. I would throw my hair out my window and some random handsome man would climb up, hold me, love me, and give me everything I have ever wanted. *Barbie's Rapunzel* was my favorite movie growing up for a reason. I had it on VHS and would watch that and *Cinderella 2* on repeat. I remember I had an entire bin of princess VHSs under my bed at my mom's house. She gave me everything that I needed to dream big... if only I never lost that room.

A hard pill I had to swallow recently, right around when I turned 26, was that no one is going to come and save me, especially not some random man... on a horse. I've learned that if I want something, I was going to have to go and get it for myself — be my own Prince Charming.

But still, that is easier said than done. I am an anxious little love bug at the end of the day, always have been. Which I guess is really just a cute way to say "love addict." I constantly crave the touch and company of a man. It's like I need it. It is torturous. And I am hyper aware of it. I wish it would just go away. So many anxious days and nights spent waiting for a call or text back. I call these feelings, *The Female Yearn*. And I know that I am not the only one out here that struggles with these feelings, but fuck, I wish they would STOP. So again, I find myself wishing I were a vampire and could turn my feelings *off*.

Addiction creeps into almost every part of my life.

I developed physically very young, aka big tits and hips, which means I started being sexualized very young. I still remember to this day all the comments that older boys, sometimes men, would make about me. Especially at summer camp. It was demoralizing, but somehow, I was trained to like it and *want more*. So, needing validation from these (creepy) men became addicting, and *habitual*.

I was in middle school when the comments became more intense. I remember I would be sitting in class and could hear boys screaming my name from the hallways. I was liked, by a lot of them, but everything they were saying about me was physical — always fucking physical. I was in seventh grade when I was first told that boys were taking my beach vacation pictures and masturbating to them. I was told this to my face, by the masturbators themselves. And for some reason, I found it flattering. And I needed *more*. I was in the eighth grade when it became a normal thing at parties for a guy in my class to pin me down on the ground and start "type writing" on my chest. He called it "typewriter time," and everyone would just stand around and watch, and laugh. I screamed the first time it happened, but then it became normal. He was also one of the masturbators, go figure. Ever since then, my body has felt like a weapon used against me. And for some fucking reason, I convinced myself to like it... and want *more*.

I thought I had the comments and attacks under control. That is until alcohol walked into the picture. And after that first night of blackout sex, I never treated myself, or my body, the same. I became an open wound of complete disassociation. An open target to be used and abused, by myself and others. I am not blaming any specific person, but I am definitely blaming a series of patterns that allowed people to touch and enter me without permission. It is such a gray area to talk about the assault you experience while drunk, especially blackout drunk, but some nights it really was just that — assault and rape. I could feel it in the mornings. And I still feel it... every single day. It's like a hollow and empty feeling, but with pressure. I don't know how to fully describe it in the physical form, but the energy is consuming. I just could never figure out why it kept happening to me and not everyone else. I subconsciously felt like a target, but when I would wake up after one of those bad nights, I could only ever blame myself. I never wanted to be a victim, but sometimes there is just no way around the truth.

Assault is confusing when you don't mentally remember it, because your body still does. It is so challenging to deal with because there is no one else to blame but yourself. You are left there, alone, to feel it all. I don't even know the faces or names of most of my abusers, but my body does, my body went through it. Again, I am not saying that every drunk hook up I have had was assault, absolutely not. But I would say at least half of them were. And that is really fucking hard to try and comprehend. I have so many open wounds that need closing, wounds that I do not even know are possible of closing. Sometimes I even question if I was just a free sex worker for all those years. And that's an even scarier thought.

However, one thing I do know is — I will never have to go through it again, at least not on my account. And that is enough for me to start to heal. I could not start healing until I quit drinking. That was the one requirement. My true abuser was alcohol, not those men. The only consistent factor was always *alcohol*.

My power is coming back to me now, but I am nowhere near perfect. I still struggle with extreme attachment and love addiction. I have used sex as a form of self-harm for years, while also "falling in love" with every man that entered me and showed me some form of "attention." I became obsessed with the pain and search for validation. But it wasn't until I started writing this book with a sober mind where I discovered a rabbit hole of memory, understanding, and forgiveness for myself. Learning about my broken heart has been the first step in my recovery, with a long way to go.

My Broken Heart

I have a broken heart. I have for a while now. I try to think back to the first person that broke it. I always thought it was my parents, because they're the easiest to blame considering how I never felt protected. Then I decided it was alcohol because, sure, alcohol caused *a lot* of my heartbreak. Alcohol was my first consistent heartbreaker, but it was not my first ever.

In 2023, while writing this book, I had a shocking, suppressed memory come back. One I wish I could throw away and never have to face again. One I wish I could go back and save my little self from.

So yes, I guess I am a victim. One in three of us are, and probably more if we are being honest.

I was so terrified when I remembered. I cried for days. But I also felt relieved. It was as if for the first time I knew, for sure, that all the abuse I experienced was not my fault.

Also, I finally understood why I have been so damn scared to touch my own vagina for 26 years. I was traumatized. I went straight to my therapist and I learned more about suppressed memories and how we can store these *really* painful experiences to try and forget. But the thing is, you never really forget, your body always recalls. Your nervous system knows. And someday, you might wake up in the middle of the night screaming because you finally *remember*.

So, for all you readers — there is usually a reason why some people, especially young girls, come off as "extra sexual," "promiscuous," or "sexually advanced." This way that they (we) act is not a strive for attention, but a programming. We are acting out of trauma — and trauma makes you easy prey. When you are sexually abused at a young age, your brain develops an attachment to that abuse. This was not an easy pill for me to swallow, but it was the start of being able to forgive myself. I never *wanted* to be someone that experienced sexual assault, but the truth is... I am. And once I started drinking, I was even more receptive to that abuse, and that's when it began to compound.

But hey, *I still believe in love.*

Finding Love Pre-quitting

Since I was in kindergarten, I have always had a love interest — whether that be a boyfriend or a crush. I have always wanted to share my everyday life and thoughts with someone, someone whom I would also like to kiss. What could be better? But what I have learned is that since I love deeply, I also feel the pain of losing love just as much, if not worse. And that can feel like death. Especially when you fuck it all up because of a bad blackout.

There is nothing worse than the morning after a bad blackout, not remembering what you did, but what you did made you lose the person that you yearn for so deeply. My big heart contributed to the deep depressions that I would go into after a bad blackout. So many hungover mornings were spent crying, days filled with regret and anger. I wanted love so bad but kept doing scary shit blacked out that would scare men off, and ruin things.

When I remove all distractions, I have a massive feeling of loneliness inside of me. It's like I know that there is supposed to be another half of my heart, but it's not there. It feels gone, hollow, and empty. I want to be complete on my own, and I work so hard to try and be, but deep down I know that I crave connection. And for so long I tried to fill that connection with any boy that could fit. So, combine that deep yearning with binge drinking, and you have a woman on a mission. A mission of finding love in the darkest place possible — a bar.

When I got drunk, I became lifeless. That is not attractive, physically nor spiritually. Who would want to enter a partnership with someone like that? I know now that drinking was not the key to me finding love, but I kept trying to make it be, over and over again. I was always searching for love at the bottom of a bottle, but all I ever found was pain.

Going out always had one goal — find someone to hook up in hopes they will love me and want to be my new boyfriend afterwards. I am what you would call a "relationship girl" at heart. I crave loyalty and partnership. I tried to fight it for years, wanting to accept myself as someone that freely fucks random people happily, but that's just not me. All random sex ever did was leave me sadder and feeling more alone. But I thought that that was how I would do it, how I would find "the one." Instead, all I found were soulless nights met with early morning regret. So please, learn it from me: *You do not find love by being blacked out at a bar. The guy that finds you in that state is NOT the "one."* I have learned this the hard way, I promise.

By the time I was eighteen, I couldn't count how many people I had slept with. I couldn't count because I didn't fucking know, and I still don't. So many nights were blurred or blacked out. Also, trying to confirm if you had sex with someone the morning after is the fucking worst, so I just avoided any conversation most of the time.

This part of my life doesn't even feel real anymore. But still, I have had to accept it. My past is also the reason I want to scream at and punch every lame ass dude that talks about body count. Like sir, "DOES RAPE COUNT TOWARDS BODY COUNT?!" Fucking uneducated and unexperienced *pussy boys*. I hope your stupid podcasts get cancelled!

I digress.

Fortunately, I met my first love when I was 21 and his name is Kareem. I had just come home from Europe and we met outside of a bar in the South Side of Pittsburgh. I wasn't too drunk that night — it was one of the good ones. I was standing outside of the Flats (iykyk) waiting for my friend, who was blacked out taking rides with random men on motorcycles that looked like they were straight out of *Duck Dynasty* (a story for another day). Once I saw him walking my way, I knew I needed to know him. I looked at him walking by and said, "Why is your shirt wet? Are you sweating?" My game was questionable, but he must have liked it because that night changed my life. Kareem saved me in a way. He taught me that I was capable of being loved. And so, from ages 21-24, I was safe. I was safe from creepy guys in bars and loveless sex.

Kareem and I very rarely had drunk sex, because I literally turned into a lifeless zombie. It was something he told me he wished we had more of in our relationship, but he is a good man and knew that when a woman can't walk or talk straight, you probably should not be having sex with her. This just puts into perspective how fucked up it was that so many random people had sex with me while I was lifeless. And so, for the next few years — I was *safe*.

Kareem

Kareem. He changed my life. We were together for years and while my drinking was still *extreme*, it was a little better when I was with him. I felt protected. He taught me what it was like to be loved by a man, unconditionally. That man would have given me his left arm if I asked him to. I once had a runny nose and he literally took his shirt off and gave it to me to blow my nose with. I really believed he would have done anything for me. I was so in love.

And then in 2021, we broke up. That sucked. Love sucks sometimes. But still, he is a huge reason I was able to quit drinking. He opened up my heart.

And now, he is one of my mirrors when it comes to staying sober. That man saw how extreme my drinking was but never made me feel bad for it. He carried me to bed like a baby almost every night during the last year of our relationship. I don't remember falling asleep for an entire year, but I always woke up tucked in nicely in our bed. He cared for me in ways that no one else ever had. When I was off my meds and couldn't get out of bed, he was there. He would do anything he could to try and make me feel better, even when it felt impossible. He saw it all and still loved me no matter what. That is something I will never forget.

He also broke up with me. That was a horrible day. I flew to Vegas within two hours. Classic Elli running style. He told me it was for me, but I just couldn't understand *why*.

Turns out, he was right. That breakup was important. A new Elli was born after. He always seemed to know exactly what I needed. I was just so co-dependent on him that I had honestly forgotten to focus on myself. And he knew that, so he gave me the greatest gift... he let me go.

It was not easy at first. My entire future felt like it died. I felt grief. I lost my best friend. I lost my protector. I also lost my drunk babysitter which meant I lost the safety net of never being taken advantage of again.

And sadly, the patterns continued shortly after he was gone.

I didn't want to be alone, so I started letting strangers into my bed. There was a major difference this time though, and that was that I knew it wasn't love.

Kareem showed me what love was. These other men were nothing but monsters, feeding.

The silver lining of it all is that if things did not play out like they did, I don't know if I would have ever quit drinking. Having Kareem meant I could drink and do whatever I wanted. Not having him meant I was in danger. And that was a scary wake up call. Once the sex patterns started happening again and I was back in situations where I am not fully saying yes and asking myself questions like, "Did I want to have sex with him?" "Did we have sex?" "He said I gave great head, I gave him head?" And so, I finally got the motivation I needed to really consider if this is a lifestyle I could have for the rest of my life. The answer was no, and if I wanted to change my life — I had to do it alone.

Within a year of our breakup, I was alcohol-free, acting, and writing daily. Three things that I never would have known I was capable of if I didn't have to sit in that apartment alone, that we once shared, and have a *really* hard look in the mirror.

Love changes. People change. But what I do know is that my first love was a gift — something that not everyone can say. And for that, for him, I am forever grateful.

Extra Info: I have always felt more comfortable with black men. I think a reason for this is because I have only ever been really hurt or taken advantage of by a white man. Isn't that something?

My mom also had a few black boyfriends (and fiancés) when I was growing up and I loved them. These men were nice and loving to me, sometimes even more so than my real dad at the time. So, yeah, it's just the way I am and what makes me feel comfortable.

Then there's also the fact that the black community has **always** accepted and welcomed me with open and loving arms. Some of my closest girlfriends to this day are black women, and I am beyond grateful to have spent so much intimate time within their culture.

Over the years, I've also learned about my own implicit biases and mistakes that I have made. My work and education to be better is never ending, and it should be this way for all of us white folks. It is our responsibility to educate ourselves and others when we can.

Quick Tip: The best way to educate yourself is to have honest and open conversations with people within the culture, *not* random shit you find online.

Just Being Honest

Why is it nearly impossible to be a sexually liberated and curious girl without someone trying to take that power away from you? Or trying to abuse you to the point of losing that power?

I have always been interested in sex. Which means I have always been overly *sexualized*. Why does it have to be like that?

Why does being considered "sexual" have to be an uncomfortable *thing* in most environments? And why does it have to negatively impact those of us who are?

Maybe I just have an aura that screams "try to fuck me" because even homeless guys whip their dicks out and start jacking off in front of me. I always thought that was a normal thing to happen until I casually mentioned it to someone in my mid-20's and they were like, "Um... no." It's not just me, right?

I do believe things are getting better in this world, or at least I like to believe that. But what is it with wanting to overpower those of us who are comfortable with our sexuality? How can we make a change?

I wish I stopped my drinking sooner. I knew it was wrong for me. But I continued to put myself out there, over and over again. Why did my body feel like it didn't belong to me for so long? When it got down to business, was I even there? Did I make sounds? How could I be present for something so intimate and not remember it? Why would someone want to be with someone like that? Was I pretending to enjoy it? Did I enjoy it? Or was I just passed out and someone was there... just fucking me? My questions are endless. And dark.

Honestly, I don't think I even want to know the answers.

The only consistent factor was that every morning when I woke up not knowing who I had sex with, my heart broke — over and over, more each time. Slowly ripping to shreds.

I have chosen to not blame anyone for what's happened, including myself. I am not perfect, never was. What I do blame though is *alcohol.*

And just like Kat Williams said, "Anything that takes away your free will is the *devil.*"

Not drinking is lonely.

Sometimes I feel like Rapunzel, minus Prince Charming, up in my apartment. I was alone a lot as a child, so you would think that I have gotten used to it by now, but no — drinking and going out were great distractions.

Another toxic pattern that I have had to face is that I have used men to try and escape my loneliness. Thinking it will be fixed by a partner who wants to see me all the time, text me all day, and be my *everything.*

Turns out, this tactic has only left me feeling even more alone. And constantly waiting for someone to give you something that they can't is exhausting. Only I can save myself from my loneliness, and this is something I am still learning today.

Now, when the pain is unbearable, I pull out my iPad and start typing away. I write through my loneliness now.

And what I have discovered is: *Loneliness is powerful.*

We should not fear loneliness. I say this with grace because I, in fact, still do fear it, but my relationship with it is getting stronger day by day. I spend a lot of time alone now. Sure, sometimes I cry about it, but then there are times that I feel myself falling in love with the solitude.

As time goes on, I know for damn sure that I would rather be lonely and alone than lonely and stuck with the wrong person. Because, let me be clear, you do not have to be alone to be lonely.

There is power in solitude, this I know now. But let's be real, I still really do want love.

Finding Love Post-Drinking

I feel like I am finding love in different ways every single day now — just not the romantic kind. Sure, I have had flings and a few fuck boys have gotten close, but I haven't been committed to someone while writing this book, and I think it needed to be this way. I needed the ability to be completely alone and... honest.

The modern dating culture is terrifying. These dating apps are scary. I am not meant for the "streets." The streets almost killed me. I always wished I could be a polyamorous and open queen, but I am not. I am monogamous to the core. I'm a Taurus — we don't like to share. I also think a major reason for all my failed attempts at love, thus far, is because I keep choosing *challenging men*, or men who have zero interest in anything other than sex. Must be my daddy issues talking. Plus, not all men can handle someone like me. I speak my mind and I don't let shit slide — ever. I also always know when someone is lying to me. Call me *psychic*.

Now, I won't settle until I find someone that is able to treat me as well, if not better, than I treat myself. And that is going to be hard, because I love myself. I take *great* care of myself. I understand why I couldn't find love for all those years... I didn't love myself. You cannot receive without having something to give, and I had nothing to give. I thought I did, but I didn't — it was obvious. I was fighting to fill this deep void in myself that could only be faced when brought to the surface. So, in order to be with me, it's going to take someone who has done that work for themselves too.

I think what ended up happening was after I quit drinking, all the love I was looking for appeared within me. All the love I ever needed, for all those years, was... in me. I thought this was crazy at first too, but it happened.

Loss of potential partnership sucks, but that is a normal feeling. What's not normal is waking up with an odd feeling down below to find out you fucked a random guy outside a bar. That is not normal. None of the horrendous experiences I had from ages 15-25 were normal. And I just really hope that anyone living like that can take a step back and consider if it's the life they want to be living. I got through with no unwanted babies or diseases, not everyone is as lucky. We need to protect ourselves.

I've been through a lot of heartbreak and pain for a 26-year-old, but I also know that I am still a young woman, learning. At least now I know that when something ends, it is not the *end*. Life really can work in your favor, if you allow it. Remember: "*If not that, then better.*"

Danger

When I go out now alcohol-free, I see how creepy and weird people get when drunk. They are like vultures looking for their next kill. It's honestly scary and I just want to scream because I know that I was one of the highest playing contestants in that game for so long.

Most men cannot handle a woman that is sober and aware, especially at a bar, and especially when that someone is me — who suffers from extreme facial expressions. I am not everyone's cup of tea, and I don't want to be. And I just want to hit these drunk people sometimes. They can be so mean! Some don't even know how to talk. I wonder what it was like to meet Blackout Elli. Actually, no, I don't want to know.

But really, being completely present, aka no alcohol, with someone you are just getting to know, on an intimate level, is... challenging. There is no buffer, no escape, and nothing to make you "loosen up." It is complete presence. And that is hard for our social media, hide behind your phone, generation.

I wish I could share every single horror story from my recent sober dating experiences, but this book is already getting too long. For now, here are some tips:

WHAT I HAVE LEARNED DATING ALCOHOL-FREE:

1. Natural hallucinogenic drugs *cough cough shrooms* affect how you feel around someone for the first time. Be careful when taking them on first dates, even as a microdose. He might try to force you into a

threesome. (Yes, this happened.)

2. Instagram photos are not always accurate. Sometimes someone's head will be a lot smaller in person and not proportional to their steroid infused body. These men are also typically aggressive, please move with caution.

3. Big dicks are not worth having someone that's a dick attached to them. (Still learning this one, I love big dicks.)

4. We are all confused and have too much information and too many options at our fingertips. Be kind to one another.

5. Hinge is cringe — at least in Atlanta. So, be careful. A homeless man might take a shower at your apartment before your second date. A car is not a home bro! (Yes, this happened. What the fuck Elli.)

6. If there comes a point where you feel like the guy in your bed is blocking you from meeting your husband, loose him.

7. If shit's not working, shit's not working. Cut your losses and move on. Always remember: *If not that, then better.*

8. There are a lot of sad men out here, which is okay. What is *not* okay is becoming their "mommy." That man needs therapy, not your vagina. (They get these two confused sometimes.)

9. Try not to have sex on the first date, it always pays off. (Still learning this one too.)

10. If he shows (or even tells) you who he is, fucking listen. You are not his savor. We can only ever save ourselves.

I digress.

My shadow of love: Who are we without our **shadow selves**? We all have one. That's the funny thing these days, everyone is so scared to be honest about it. Why are we so scared of our demons? Don't we know that if we actually connect on them, then we can tackle them together? Why do we have to pretend to be these perfect people? Romantic partnerships bring out the best... and worst in humans, so why hide?

I believe that once people are able to be more authentic, then maybe relationships will work better. Not everyone is meant to be monogamous, and that is okay. But why lie? Also, this internet bullshit is just not fucking cutting it for me. No one has a perfect life. No. Fucking. One. So please, let's just be fucking real. And remember, *we are only as sick as our secrets.*

Also, everyone wants love, so let's stop trying to play it cool and act like we don't. Most wars were fought over a vagina, ya know. I digress... yet again.

27

The Married Man

Okay, it's story time again folks. I said that I attract some of the most mysterious men, right?

Well, the Married Man was one of them.

It was the summer of 2021, a few months after my breakup, post-pandemic, and I was a Premium Account Executive for a professional basketball team, aka I was courtside for every game. The team was in the playoffs and we were finally back to full capacity. Things were lit in Atlanta, and it felt like the world was my oyster.

It was right at the peak of summer when this particular man came into my life. Safe to say that the world was already moving fast, but this man made it move even faster. Lightning speed. And one of the most interesting periods of my life thus far was right ahead of me.

He was a frequent courtside client of mine that would sneak me drinks while I was working. Every Sprite can that I was carrying around the arena that year always had at least two shots of Hennessey in it. And I was having multiple "Sprites" per night. I was living. Definitely could have been fired, but certainly *living*. Post games were the best. I was drinking in the courtside club with celebrities, for FREE. Wait, no, I was getting paid to be there, so even better. It was the first time I saw *real* money. Also the first time I started making some real money. I do have to thank the Married Man for some of my sales, he introduced me to a few of my highest paying clients. But really, I need to thank the Sprites. Those drinks helped a bitch sell.

Those nights were then followed by countless strip clubs, cool underground events, interesting "business meetings", *blackouts*, and so much more.

For a short period of time, I was basically in a "relationship" with him. All his friends knew me, we went out all the time, but still... he was married. This chapter is not one of my proudest moments, but hey, he did say that his wife knew about me and our relationship. So back then, that was enough for me.

Everywhere we went — bottle service. He even got my mom and I bottle service once. It was the night that one of my other clients let me use his tickets to take my mom to her first courtside game. That was the last time my mom and I drank together, and it was a good night. I am thankful for that. I even have some drunk pictures courtside with her and Saucy Santana. So fun.

I fell in love with Atlanta that summer. Going to Pink Pony at 1 p.m. on a Tuesday and ordering a bottle of $300 wine just to sit and watch some guys conduct a "business meeting" is an experience that I think everyone should have. Given, I never paid for anything, at least not until the end when things got bad, but there were still about 20 fully paid visits to the strip clubs where I had a good ass time, at least from what I can remember. Atlanta is amazing, and it finally felt like home.

Fun fact: When I closed my first 100k+ sale with the professional basketball team, I submitted the contract while sitting at Cheetah with the Married Man, sipping on another $300 bottle of wine, as he conducted one of thus "business meetings." It was noon on a Tuesday. Post-covid was a wild time, huh?

However, things did not end great for us. They usually don't in these types of scenarios. But that is not the point of this story. The point is that this relationship was one of the major turning points in my life with drinking. The Married Man was no stranger to alcoholism, and he saw that I had a problem. He helped me become more aware of my drinking problem in a way that no one had before. He never told me to quit, but always mentioned that I *could* if I wanted to. He wanted to help me, but he also knew that you don't quit by being told to quit. He was an experienced fighter with alcoholism. He was also the first person to teach me that you don't need to drink to be cool. Until then, I had always thought alcohol made me "cooler," but he taught me that it actually does quite the opposite. And that was tough to hear over and over again.

He taught me to replace every other drink with a sparkling water and lemon. Sounds small, but that shit helped. Sure, I didn't listen half the time, but still, no one ever taught me shit like that, they only ever taught me how to drink *more.* He told me about times when he would go six months without drinking and felt amazing. Little did I know, my mind was getting programmed every time he mentioned it. He was a huge help. So, if you are reading this Married Man, thank you.

So, ya, no matter what happened, it all needed to happen. And for that I am grateful — now time for the actual story.

The Night My Apartment Turned Into A Whore House

It was August 2021 when "Club Elli" opened. The day started normally — riding with the Married Man in his BMW to the local strip club, Pink Pony, at 1 p.m. We got in the club and sat with a few of his friends who were also with their "girlfriends." All of these damn men were married, ugh — but I might as well be honest. And again, not my finest moment. After a few hours at the club, I put together that some of the Married Mans friend's "girlfriends" were also "retired" strippers. And they wanted to dance. So of course, in Drunk Elli fashion, I invited everyone back to my apartment.

This is when things got interesting. Bear with me, I do not remember the whole night, but there was some video footage and I was able to piece parts of it together. Once we were all back at my apartment the men whipped out at least 20k in ones and those women were butt naked within two minutes, dancing, all over my living room. I took some more shots because, ANXIETY, obviously, and then I remember just sitting there and watching, vividly. It was fascinating.

Worth a mention — I love strippers, but I don't like touching strippers. I love women, but I don't want to slap their asses. I just want to admire them, pat them on the back, and then say, "Hey, take all this money before he looks back over here," and then slide as much as I can fucking salvage for them. I love giving them money, especially when it's not mine. They fucking deserve it. Strippers are smart, and I love smart women.

I don't remember much after their clothes were off, that's usually when I would walk away, but I do remember the entire floor of my apartment being covered in ones. And then my friend, X, called. She was down the street having a fight with one of her girlfriends. *Apparently*, I said something convincing and got her to drive over to my spot. I don't think she was expecting to walk into what she did, but what I do know is that she immediately forgot about that fight with her girlfriend — at least for those few hours. That's how feral it was. I sadly don't remember much after that, but the Married Man did send me a video the next day of Buns and I sitting in my sunroom away from everyone, staring out the window, and then it panned over to the other side of my apartment, which was butt ass naked women grinding (possibly fucking) one of the guys... on my couch.

I tell this story to show the levels of IDGAF I got to when drinking. But honestly, I would have probably hosted this gathering sober. I prefer to live a life that is free — where others, and myself, can be our natural, unhinged, and wild selves. And this night was just that... freedom.

Also, I was able to help a dear friend in need forget her problems for the night. What else are friends for?

The months following were pretty much the same — money, sex, and partying. So, I guess you could say that I had an *adventurous* last year of drinking. However, little did I know, I was growing into the woman that would leave all of this behind in less than a year, and by May 4th, 2022 — Club Elli had officially *closed*.

28

FEMALE LOVES

Something that I am learning more with age is that there are no relationships more important than those with my close girlfriends. They are the ones that are there for it all — good and bad. It is so easy, *especially as a lover girl*, to get consumed by a man. But after learning the hard way, I know that pouring my love into my friendships will always bring the greatest reward.

NOT some random man you meet online and create false fantasies about. NO. That man is just trying to fuck you. Your girlfriends are not trying to fuck you. They actually love you. And NOT that hot other man that messages you on IG at midnight saying, "I give it three months until you're my wife." NO. It's actually three months until he ghosts you, bitch. (Clearly talking to myself here.) But yeah, love takes time. Love takes energy. And for me, the most rewarding love comes from all of the amazing women in my life.

Some people, mostly men in my case, are just meant to be speed bumps. They are there to make you stop, re-adjust, slow down, and then keep moving forward. Maybe leaving a possible scratch or two, but nevertheless, you always keep moving forward — more cautiously each time. Sometimes you may run over the speed bump a little too quickly, injuring you both, but again, that's how you learn. There is nothing *wrong* with speed bumps, but you really should learn to move with caution around them. And if one of them beats you up a little too much, just take a different damn street next time.

Okay, back to the ladies. There are a few women, already in the spotlight, that have had a major influence on my work. They have helped me nurture the confidence I needed to share my own story, and my dedications to two of these women are as follows.

Dear Lena Dunham,

It was 2018 when I first discovered who you were. I had just finished my six-month study abroad semester in Prague, where I partied harder and longer than ever before. It was basically a six-month bender and I almost died a few times. But that's not important for this letter, what's important is that in May 2018, while finishing out thus euro trip, I discovered your book *Not That Kind of Girl*. It was in a bookstore near one of the museums in Vienna — what a beautiful area that was. This book was different. This book stood out. I felt connected to you instantly and I was beyond excited to start it. So, I headed to a park near my Airbnb and sat down on a bench in front of a large, beautiful church. I actually took a picture of the exact spot I was sitting and have it hanging up in living room as I write this. And Lena, I did not leave that bench until I finished your damn book. I don't even know how long it took, but I sat there from start to finish — no breaks. That's only happened to me a few times in my life, reading a book start to finish, and it was usually those books in high school that we had summer reading for and I procrastinated and *had* to binge read. But yours was different, yours changed me with each page that I flipped, and I couldn't put it down.

For so long I had felt alone, but reading your book was the first time that I felt like I wasn't. Long story short, my childhood was lonely and I have a binge drinking problem. I was actually in a pretty deep drinking depression when I found your book. I am 26 now while writing this, in a much better headspace, as I quit drinking at 25, but this book saved me when I was *not* doing well. I was drowning in shame and constantly asking myself questions like, "What is wrong with me?" "Why am I like this?" "Why does no one love me?" But on that bench, I wasn't alone anymore — I found you. You have a voice that I understood. A voice that made me feel seen. Your book gave me a sense of security I had never had before. Nothing was wrong with me, I was just different. And different is *good*. Different can write a fucking *book*.

It was the raw honesty and the "get dirty and real" that finally made me feel comfortable in my own skin. I remember reading it and being like, "Holy shit that happened to me too!" or "Oh my God, this girl!" Haha. But truly, you started a path for women to be their honest and real selves. And for that, I am grateful. It's interesting, I was in Vienna for ten days alone and it was the least alone I had felt in years. Your book opened something in my mind, and now six years later, I am telling my story in hopes to impact others just like you did me. You are a major inspiration for my book and telling my story, so I need to properly thank you. Thank you, Lena.

But that's not it because then, when I made it back to the US, I discovered *Girls*. *Girls*... is a fucking masterpiece, Lena. *Girls* is the truth of the human experience for 20 something year-old women. I have watched it probably 4-5 times in the last few years and have also read your book a few times — not to be creepy, you just *GET IT*.

You are fabulous and I pray that one day you and I are able to meet, and hopefully I can learn even more from you. I hope to influence young women, and men, I guess old too, just like you did me. You've led this path for a while now. I hope to continue it with you.

xoxo,
Elli Rose

Dear Julia Fox (aka Mother),

You have single handedly made me feel sexier in my own skin. Breaking addiction is sexy. And so are you.

I was recently listening to the interview of you talking about your book, post publish, and you were asked about that one video that went viral of you calling your book a "masterpiece" with that big ass eyeliner (slay).

During the interview, you said that when that video was released, you actually hadn't even started writing your book yet. This made me laugh out loud. You then said that because that video went viral, you then had to lock yourself away to actually write the book. Well, it's funny because when that video went viral, it also motivated me to get my shit together and finishing writing this book, so, thank you.

I preordered your book, obviously. I was counting down the damn days and girl, I LOVE it. More than love, *oh my lord!* You pushed me. I had to tell more of my truth after reading yours. Your story helped me become more real and raw in my own writing about the dark place's addiction has taken me.

Your stories felt familiar. And you helped me judge myself less. Other people's stories help. Hearing stories you can relate to, even with massive differences, *helps.* Also, now I feel proud for overcoming all the shit I have gone through, not ashamed — because I came out of it. There is so much beauty in pain.

It also takes a lot of love and a *need* to help people to put all your baggage out there. It's also sometimes the only way to get people to listen. People listen to you.

Sure, we all have flaws, but it takes balls to put them out there. You have balls. I also have balls. We both have balls.

Wanna hang out? Text me.

xoxo,

Elli Rose

29

Bigger Than Me: Spirit

Alcohol is a powerful spirit. It had me doing shit you would not even believe. I faced a lot of darkness during my drinking years, not only during the blackouts, but also those mornings after. I was constantly fighting myself — my shadow self.

What I wish I knew then is that I should have been more welcoming and nurturing to the darker aspects of myself, rather than fighting and pushing them down with booze until I burst. But I was young, so I let the darkness consume me.

Our shadow selves will never magically disappear. And we shouldn't want them to. We should invite them in. Integrating with one's shadow is how true empowerment is felt, it is where confidence grows, and it is ultimately how consciousness extends.

Integrating with my shadow self was a key element of my journey to alcohol sobriety. I needed to accept the darker aspects of myself. And although it was and still is hard, it is through the pain and in the darkness where I find my *magic*.

But before I knew all of this, I was still playing with fire every night.

I read somewhere that the word alcohol stems from the Arabic word "Al-Kuhl," which means *body-eating spirit*. Then I read that the English root of alcohol is "ghoul," which is an evil demon that eats human bodies...? Um... what the fuck?

So, basically, alcohol extracts the soul from the body and eats it — which is why I say I lived most of my life in darkness. It destroys the spirit. Oh, and don't forget that it is killing brain cells in the process... cherry on top.

Our bodies are vessels for our spirits, and when alcohol is involved, we open up our vessels for the "ghouls" to enter. One sip of alcohol could change everything. Usually not the first sip, but that one sip that takes it too far, and then — *poof* — memory gone. Walking and talking like a creepy blacked out zombie. Blackout Elli was haunting. I was letting "Al-Kuhl" take the wheel. And **that** is why people change when they drink.

Ultimately, spirituality is what saved me. We all deserve to believe in whatever spirit or God we want, even if that choice is nothing. It took me time to *discover* what kind of spiritual practice fits into my life. However, once I did, I soon realized that I had been practicing it my entire life. I just have more tools and direction now.

I practice spiritual energy work — think Reiki, tarot and oracle cards, energy healing, basically all the "witchy shit." Through these practices I find my answers and speak to my higher powers. When drinking, I was suppressing this power. My *frequency* was low. That's what drinking does, it lowers your *frequency*.

Then, when you quit, sure, you may be bored at first, but then you slowly start to enjoy everything more, and I mean *everything*. The sun shines brighter, flowers bloom more beautifully, perfume smells stronger — it's everything. Everything is enhanced. And suddenly, your frequency also rises. *Just like magic.*

So, that's what spirituality really is to me. Turning pain into magic.

In 2020, I started listening to Solfeggio frequencies on low volume every night — specifically 528 Hz (hertz). This frequency is known for helping with stress reduction, deep relaxation, and overall emotional regulation. I also believe that it helps with DNA repairing, which is the most basic building block within us. Listening to these frequencies somehow, deep in my subconscious, helped me reprogram my brain to be able to break a horrible habit.

Life is a frequency; it is constantly going up and down. Think of it like a rollercoaster. Okay, now look up what a frequency looks like (if you don't already know). You, see? Same thing. *Everything* is connected.

In order to raise your frequency, it is not about raising the highs or minimizing the lows, no. What you need to do is raise the placement of the **entire** roller coaster. Then the lowest of lows will still be higher than the previous highest of highs. And how did I do that? Well, I had to eliminate the habits and patterns in my life that lowered my frequency in the first place... starting with alcohol. Let me be clear — alcohol lowers your frequency. It is a depressant.

I operate at an entirely different frequency now. Also, I fucking love rollercoasters.

The Untethered Soul by Michael A. Singer taught me a lot about living a spiritually fulfilling life. He writes about something called the Tao, which is defined as, "the way of the universe." Taoism is difficult to define, but essentially it is living in harmony. Think of it like a pendulum swinging back and forth; Tao is when that energy is at rest in the middle. When I was binge drinking, my energy was not at rest — I was swinging to an *extreme*. Binging, blacking out, regretting it, feeling bad, searching for more alcohol, finding another event, binging again, and so on and so forth. Not at rest.

Then when I initially quit, I was also not at rest nor in harmony. I was still swinging, just all the way to the other side. Chugging Diet Cokes, smoking boat loads of weed, excessively picking myself apart, word vomiting, self-isolating, and so on. However, somehow, somewhere, while dancing with both extremes for extended periods of time, there was just one day when I suddenly fell into what felt like harmony — the Tao.

How? Well, I feel it when I am writing this book. The more that I read and write about alcoholism, the more I understand my struggles and what I have gone through. And trying to understand this concept of "Taoism" helped me face the truth that I am still not perfect without alcohol, and I never will be. Which somehow lead me to peace — to the Tao.

I'm not even sure if I have comprehended this whole concept correctly, so I definitely recommend reading the book yourself, but whatever I did comprehend helped me. And I am grateful for that. Maybe that's what will happen with this book. People might not fully understand it, but they will still become a better version of themselves after it. I sure have.

I would have never found my form of "the Tao" without removing alcohol from my life. Never. I'm sure there are many more struggles coming my way that will throw my equilibrium off balance, but nothing will ever take me back to who I was when I was drinking.

The Untethered Soul also touches on a concept called samskaras. Samskaras are described as, "balls of undigested emotions that continue to affect us." They can be programmed with specified details of our lives and can form negative thick blocks, backing up all the way to childhood. And what these samskaras need are to be cleared.

You may feel a samskara activate when your heart starts beating fast after you see something or someone that triggers a past event in your life. Let's say that when you were a teenager, some guy touched you inappropriately. You didn't do anything about it in the moment, but that feeling of invasion stuck. Then say a few years later you are out getting coffee with a friend and you see someone who looks *just* like the guy that touched you. Well, now you have this overwhelming negative feeling that you just can't explain. You try to shake it off and forget about it, but later that night when you're lying with your partner and they start to touch you, you snap. You don't fully know why but you just feel triggered. And now your partner is hurt and you don't even know what to say or why you acted that way because you shoved the painful memory so deep down into your subconscious.

Well, what really happened is earlier at the coffee shop a massive chunk of negative energy, that had been stored where that man touched you, was triggered. When you saw the look-alike at the coffee shop, you felt paralyzed. *That* is a blocked samskara.

In order to clear samskaras, you're going to need to meditate. At least that's what I have been doing. I am still figuring this whole concept out myself. And y'all... let's just say I have enough negative samskaras to traumatize an entire town. So, go ahead and do yourself a favor by searching, "how to clear negative samskaras." That's what I do.

The concepts I covered in this chapter have helped me, but I also understand that this language is not for everyone.

Again, this is my *diary.*

30

Marketing of Alcohol & The Prohibition

Have you ever taken a step back and wondered why the most exciting birthday celebration is usually 21? Think about it.

Why? Well, it's probably because we live in a society that presents going out to a bar and legally getting a drink as the highlight of one's life experience. I was guilty myself; I couldn't wait to turn 21. The thought of being able to go out drinking, without the constant stress of getting caught, felt like I was finally about to live. But turns out, going out and being able to drink did nothing but make my life harder. Why? Because now I was able to access my *poison* whenever, and however, I wanted.

It is not my intention to put down anyone who likes to go out and get a drink or safely enjoys the spirit at home. My intention is to bring attention to how much control and power alcohol has over the human race, especially those who cannot control it. And the fact that it is shoved down our throats on a daily basis... not cool.

Before I was 21, I had to be sneaky and smart in order to drink. Well, I turned 21 while living in Prague, so my birthday (in my head) was the minute that plane landed in Europe, which was a few months prior to my actual birthday. This is actually an interesting perspective because I remember not even caring about my birthday since I already had everything I needed. My first "legal" drink was that first night in Prague — a few friends and I landed on no sleep, quickly unpacked in our new dorms, and immediately went out to the nearest bar to chug beers. That was a good night. I didn't blackout that night, which was typically not the case in Europe.

What I am trying to say is that we give this age so much power because we are finally able to go out and drink, but for those of us who are addicts, this is the beginning of a very challenging life. From having to sneak and hustle alcohol, to being able to walk into any store and buy it… deadly. At least it was for me, but I still continued to do it for years. Why? Because it was too fucking easy.

I can guarantee that at some point in every person's life they have seen alcohol negatively affect themselves or someone they love. But have you ever seen it help anyone? Have you ever seen it be the sole reason that someone did something amazing and life changing, in a good way? Sure, it gives "confidence" and "courage," but these are falsified versions. What happens when you wake up the next day and you feel shy and quiet? Well, then you have to go drink again to feel those things — and that's where they get you. Now you are reliant on this *thing* that you need in order to feel how you want to feel. It's a fucking trap.

Alcohol is everywhere. It controls people, the economy, and really the world. What would happen if everyone stopped drinking? The economy would plummet. *They* don't want that. So, *they* will keep pushing and selling it.

Alcohol is a poison. It ruins lives and has done so for thousands of years. So why is it still the center focus of media, dining, and events? Why is it the most important ingredient to all "good parties?" Why do we continue to drink it even though we know it can kill us? Well, I think it's because we are spoon fed a dream that alcohol can make our lives better and more enjoyable when in actuality, it does the complete opposite.

The alcohol industry's marketing tactics are misleading. We are fed these beautiful commercials and ads of different alcoholic beverages paired with a lifestyle that is quite simply not realistic for most consumers. It's funny, because what they are selling is something that usually makes that desired "lifestyle" a million times farther away. I'd bet that most of those paid actors in the ads don't even drink the product they are promoting. (Just saying.)

No one runs a marathon and dedicates their accomplishment to alcohol. No one goes to the Olympics and thanks alcohol for helping them get there. No one wins an Oscar and says, "I want to thank the bottle of Tito's I drink every night." They just don't. Most of the people that are doing these great things probably put the bottle down years ago — a lot of successful people do. I even bet that most of the owners of these major alcohol brands don't even drink their own damn product, but they sure as hell make millions, if not billions, off the ones that do. Interesting, right?

Times are changing and the world is waking up. I predict that it will be illegal, or at least heavily monitored, to publicly market alcohol as a "positive" in the next few decades. If you look at the tobacco industry, you will see that they had to completely reconstruct their marketing tactics in the 70's due to the extreme negative health effects. Also, if you look at the cigarette packages in America compared to those in Europe... you will scream. I nearly lost my mind when I saw my first European cigarette package. They have like rotting toenails or dead babies on them saying something like, "consumption of this product can lead to death." Nothing like the truth, am I right?

It would be nice for alcohol brands to have to follow these same rules. It would help, especially for the younger generations to come. Personally, I would want the bottles to have images of people throwing up in the toilet, calling their ex fifty times, crashing their car, getting a DUI and spending time in jail, oh, and a shit ton of dried out livers. Because let's be real, all of those are real life examples of the effects of alcohol. **Not** some random hot girl giving you her number and then you pulling off in a 200k Lamborghini with a random bottle of tequila in the backseat — no.

It's not illegal to smoke cigarettes today, and Big Tobacco is clearly not out of business. They are just more honest about the real effects of their products. Again, alcohol is not deadly for everyone, some people don't have an addictive personality and can handle a few drinks. I can't. And it is still not my goal to shame anyone or any company, I am just asking for a little more honesty, ya know, so we can prevent the continuation of alcohol ruining (and ending) millions of lives — just like it almost did mine.

Alcohol would have **absolutely** ruined my life if I continued to use it how I was. If I went a day without a drink, I was proud of myself. Why was I proud? Because I knew that the shit was bad for me and that I should not be drinking it. Alcohol appears as an "easy" way out of dealing with life, but the truth is that life will **never** be easy. Drinking to feel better is simply a habit that gives its consumers an instant satisfaction of relief, as most shitty habits do. However, that instant satisfaction sets its users up for the opposite feeling and consequences long term.

I quit because I saw the positives of quitting finally outweighing not. My brain could literally no longer support the decision to live in such a system of give and take. I could no longer comprehend spending my hard-earned money on poison. I was going to the liquor store almost every day from ages 22-25. The guy at the liquor store down the street from my apartment in Atlanta always mentioned how much he loved my tattoos. It's a red flag if the clerk at the local liquor store knows your name and tattoos. Don't be that girl.

It is a systematic issue that something sold and shoved down our throats can easily ruin our lives. It takes one night to get a DUI, one night to blackout and fall, one night to fuck up your marriage. I have sat with myself and really tried to understand the benefits of alcohol — I couldn't. From my experience: it ruins everything, changes people, and makes life more difficult. It causes fights and self-harm. It causes overnight life changes that you don't remember making. It causes lack of control and depression. From a non-abuser's point of view, I could see how they could fight me on this and say, "But Elli, it helps me relax!" "Elli, it helps me get out of my shell and talk..." "Elli, it helps me sleep!" Yes, I am sure it *does*, but it also might make you accidentally kill an innocent person after you only "had a few" and "can drive," so there's that. And fuck, there are so many healthier alternatives to relax. Drink some fucking CBD! Workout. Take a nap? We don't have to continue to poison ourselves to "feel good!" No one feels good hungover. NO. ONE.

As of now, alcohol brands are allowed to promote using print, radio, television, website, and social media. They spend millions of dollars on these marketing tactics and can do so because, in return, they make billions.

But what about the Prohibition Era? I started researching the prohibition when I was already fairly deep into writing the book, which means I did not need all of this information to quit, but it definitely solidified my decision.

The Prohibition ran from January 17th, 1920, to December 5th, 1933. And the more time that passes, the more people forget about it, especially younger generations coming up. I honestly didn't know much about it until I started doing research for this book and I was born in 1997, which was only a little over 50 years post-prohibition. That is not much time.

So, why did the Prohibition start? Why did it end? Look it up... it's honestly quite interesting. I discovered something along the lines of, "to encourage drinkers to help each other resist temptation," "response to pre-existing issues like domestic violence and child abandonment whose presumed cause was alcohol," and "as a method for preventing abuse from alcoholic husbands." Like... what the fuck? And okay, so, why did the prohibition end? Yes, you guessed it — money. It's always about the mother fucking money. And honestly, I think population control might have something to do with it too.

Okay, I'm done with my history lesson on the United States because quite frankly it is not fun, and I don't want to do it anymore. But the prohibition was real, and you should do some research yourself on why it happened. The dangers of alcohol abuse are written in history. This is not a "small" deal. It is a big deal. HUGE.

I see a future without alcohol being a daily habit for most. I see a future where the truth is printed on billboards. I see a future where teenagers and young adults are properly educated about the negative side effects of alcohol. I see a future where we are taught that life is actually really beautiful without it. I **see** this for us. Not an end to alcohol, but a change. A very, *very* massive change.

2025 Note: NBA games now have non-alcoholic beverage marketing on the court. I repeat... on the motherfucking court! It's happening.

31

I Am Not Crazy

For so long I thought that I was crazy.

"Oh Elli, you're so *crazy* when you drink!" "Wow, that was really wild what you did last night, you're *crazy*!" "Omg Elli, I just heard the craziest thing about you! What were you thinking, *crazy* lady!"

Turns out, I was never crazy. I was just trying to figure out how to survive. And how I survived was to escape. And how I escaped was I found the easiest form that was also the easiest to cover up as "normal teenage behavior." That being getting belligerently drunk as frequently as possible, which typically led to "crazy" behavior.

I was hurt. Like deep rooted hurting and hatred for myself. From ages 16-21, I couldn't stand looking in the mirror. And so, I drank. I drank to the point that I couldn't see my own reflection. And then I drank more. I drank to disappear.

And I know I am not the only one with this narrative.

What I think made my situation unique is that I manipulated my pain, addiction, and depression to look *pretty*. Well, as pretty as possible. No one knew the truth or extent of what I was going through. I was hiding it. I was a chameleon. I was *acting*. Sometimes even for myself.

I was living most of my childhood in survival mode. And my complex trauma has caused me, even in my adult years, to accept much less than I deserve. It has also made it very difficult to allow myself to *enjoy* the good in life. I am constantly looking for what's next, trying to be better. Trying to be *something*. And I constantly have to remind myself that healing takes time. I am learning to quiet my mind. To think less. But again, that is hard. And I just want to feel better *now*.

Some mental illnesses can be classified as trauma responses. I might have become a completely different person without all the traumatic things that happened to me in my life, but honestly, I am happy that they did. I love myself and who I am today. And I wouldn't be here without it all. Plus, my life has blessed me with endless content.

Trauma caused my behaviors — *not* my personality. I am a survivor, not a crazy lady.

Generational Trauma

I come from a family of "crazy women." We have all been called fucking crazy.

My great-grandmother was sent to get electric shock therapy (ECT) in the 50's because she was "crazy." Really she just had severe depression, but since no one knew what to do about it, they sent her to get aggressively shocked in the head. Nice!

Okay, I am not being fully honest... she did do something naughty. What had actually happened was she caught my great-grandfather cheating on her so she stabbed him. Yeah, that's right, she stabbed him. And since he was the Chief of Police in their town and infidelity could have cost him his job, they decided to declare her as "crazy" instead and force her to get ECT. Just so he could keep his job. Please let that sink in.

No wonder I have been called crazy so much — it is a generational curse. A curse that I am now transforming into power. For too long I couldn't figure out how to make sense of my behaviors, so considering myself "crazy" was the familiar option to try. Then the more I said it, the more I believed it. Not anymore, that ends here.

32

Drinking Is A Habit

Drinking is a habit.

A habit that I lived with for ten years. It was just what I did. It was a part of my day-to-day life. I was living in a routine that included daily drinking. And then I stopped. I broke that habit. That is what I technically did when I quit drinking — I quit a habit. I need to be repetitive about this because it really is as simple as that. A habit. Recognizing alcohol, or whatever your vice may be, as a "habit that can be broken" will shift your perspective and assert that you are capable of quitting thus **habit**.

Atomic Habits by James Clear breaks down the power of habits perfectly. I actually read it for the first time when I was writing the original draft of this book, which was an absolute mess. But after I finished reading it, I was finally able to implement some sort of writing structure as a **daily habit** into my life. Basically, I told myself that in order to finish this book I had to write or edit at least 1,000 words a day. It was hard, but setting this goal worked and I have a finished-*ish* book now. Of course I missed some days or didn't hit that exact limit all the time, but the intention was set, and now I write almost every single day. I don't even have to force myself anymore. Habits are powerful. And I most definitely am a creature of habit... good and bad. That's the thing about habits, there are good ones and then there are bad ones. Positive and negative. Ying and yang. You feel me?

Environments form habits. Think about it... what makes you want to drink? Maybe hanging out with friends whom the only thing you have in common with is drinking? Maybe the bottles of wine in your kitchen that are used for "decoration?" Maybe having parents and grandparents who drink with every meal and heavily on holidays? Whatever or whoever it is, they trigger that habit. Because think about it... if they are doing it, why wouldn't you?

But it doesn't have to be this way. Sure, it's going to take some effort, but at least now you have a place to start — change your environment. Sound scary? It's not. Start small.

To start small, first look at your circle. Your "party friends" probably gotta go. It's okay, they will be fine and honestly probably won't like you as much when you're sober anyways, vice versa. You can choose to hang out with sober people. They exist. Especially in today's world. Being sober is "cool" now, and it wasn't always like that. Who you surround yourself with is going to be the #1 factor when it comes to quitting a shitty habit, especially in the beginning. It matters. Why? Because you are who you surround yourself with.

Every single morning now, I wake up feeling better than the day before. That's the compounding effect of positive habits. I swear the whole year prior to when I quit, I was slowly implementing changes in my environment because I was subconsciously setting myself up to be able to quit. I always wanted to quit, the intention was there since I was 14 watching my parents get drunk and do regrettable shit. I just had to figure out how to break the habit for myself. And I needed to remove myself from that environment. Also, content consumption. Before quitting I created a new Instagram and followed a shit ton of sober accounts that I still follow to this day. Our environment is unfortunately our phones now too. (I will get to my issues with social media later.)

Rehabs are an example of the power of a change in environment. Rehabs, specifically in-patient, work because they provide a new environment where it is easier to break habits and addictions. They work because while you are there, you have no access to your poison and are around like-minded individuals with the same goal. However, the downside of rehabs is that once you get sent home, aka put right back into the environment that made you sick, you may easily readapt back to the habits initially formed there. Changed environments change lives.

This is why I really push the fact that **you** need to be the one to change your environment. No one can force you to quit, **you** have to do it for yourself. Rehab is great if you need it to get started and are able to afford it, which is damn near impossible these days, but the best choice really is to implement the daily tactics they use in rehabs at home and make them permanent in your daily life. Not many people can afford to be sent away every few months to get better. Most of us will have to do it ourselves.

This is not me hashing rehabs, I just saw this all firsthand. My mom went to rehab when I was in high school. It worked for her at first, she was a year sober after it, but her parole officer was also testing her so she legally couldn't drink. I guess rehab did something for her, but it was also a really challenging time. It was like she was in prison and it was so hard to get ahold of her. I had like ten different numbers for the rehab center stored in my phone and would try to call them the second I got out of school, usually never being able to get ahold of her. She was also there during Christmas. That sucked.

I mention all of this because I have been on both sides of addiction, and from my experience, rehab is not the only answer. I sat through plenty of "family of addicts" meetings, but they were such a mindfuck because I was an addict then myself. It was so confusing.

The only way I was able to quit was to create the changes for myself. Sure, it took ten years, but that's because there was nothing that anyone could have said or done for me to quit, it had to be on my own terms. It was all self-research and self-effort. Watching my mom go through everything expedited my decision, of course. I saw alcohol almost ruin her life for good and that scared the shit out of me. I don't want my kids dealing with what I did, it was shitty. Addiction doesn't get better with age, **it gets worse**. The compounding effect. Also, I have said it before and I will say it again, **addiction is not our fault, but it is our responsibility**.

Atomic Habits shares an interesting story about the Vietnam War. A lot of soldiers became "addicted" to heroine during that war. However, once those men left that environment and came back to the states, where they had never used or seen heroine, most did not relapse. Using heroine was a habit that they formed in Vietnam, during an extremely traumatizing war. But once their environment changed, so did their cravings. Interesting, right?

Please know that failure is okay. I tried to quit so many times before I finally did. Those "failed" attempts always counted. Do not give up. It will stick. I am living proof that you can be an overnight success — it just might take ten years.

Another environmental change I had to make was to remove all alcohol from my home. I would not be able to think straight if there was a bottle of wine in my fridge every night. I can't have it sitting in there, it would tarnish the environment I built for myself in order to stay sober. The interesting thing though is that that is only the case for my house. Other people's houses don't bother me, that's their space. It is specifically my space — it is a boundary I have set for myself and **my** environment. *My sober environment.* That brings up another key point, you will absolutely need to set boundaries with others when it comes to changing your habits and environment, mostly with the people that you love the most. Be prepared for that.

Bad habits compound over time, but so do good ones. There is a massive difference from waking up hungover verses not. I feel good every morning now. I rarely get sick. I am happier. I have my time back. I am eating better. I smell amazing. Life is just better. I used to wake up and immediately throw up stomach acid. Now, I wake up and have a relaxing cup of coffee and then take a perfect poop. That's what I mean when I say life is more beautiful. It is more beautiful because it was so fucked up before. Be patient with yourself, but also continue to tend to your garden. The fruits of your labor can't come without the *tending*.

Drinking is also a habit of not being yourself. It fuels imposter syndrome and insecurity. Say you're an artist and you have a performance. You are nervous so you take 4-5 shots and rock the set. Yeah sure, you did a pretty good job... but you were drunk. Do you wake up feeling proud? Or do you feel disconnected from the performance? Then your next performance comes and you need to take the shots again because you have never done it without. Sure, you loosen up, but you know that it's not just you anymore. You are feeding something. You are feeding a monster that is slowly gaining control over what you love most. And truth is, you might think your performance was good, but it actually sucked in comparison to what you could have done sober.

Alcohol changes you — it is a spirit. When you wake up after those performances, you can't fully thank or be proud of just yourself because you subconsciously give alcohol credit. Drinking fuels imposter syndrome. It then leads to you losing confidence in your own capabilities and this pattern grows. You start needing more alcohol. Then you know how that story goes. Most careers don't survive a reliance on alcohol. It is a vicious fucking cycle.

Moral of the story, it feels so much better to do and accomplish things without alcohol. Sure, it will be harder at first, especially when you are doing big and scary things, but once you get used to it, and get over **normal human fears**, you realize that YOU are doing cool and badass shit, NOT alcohol. And that feels *really fucking good*. You do not need a weak ass crutch to reach peak performance, if anything that crutch is going to give out and make you plummet to a passion-death. Fuck alcohol, especially when it comes to creative abilities.

The habit of binge drinking daily will slowly, or quickly, kill you. Alcohol consumption is autocatalytic. It controls you. The reason it took years for me to quit is because I was controlled, physically and spiritually. It took time to learn and understand this information, which is exactly why I want to provide it all in one simple and easy location, this book. Easy consumption — just like alcohol, lol.

33

A Love Letter to Shameless

I could write an entire book on the accuracies of alcoholism, addiction, and mental illness depicted in the show *Shameless*. If you have not watched, please do. But for now, I will give you a brief synopsis.

Shameless, created by Paul Abbott, is about a poor family growing up in the South Side of Chicago. The dad, Frank, struggles with alcoholism and has lost complete control. He is around, but he brings disaster everywhere that he goes, so the oldest kids, Fiona and Lip, have to raise their other three siblings. The show does a fantastic job at displaying how addiction in families is passed down generation to generation.

Jeremy Allen White, who plays Lip (the eldest son), is one of my favorite actors. I relate to him a lot and he actually reminds me of one of my brothers, which is probably why he and his interactions with his siblings feel so familiar. And then there is Fiona (the eldest daughter) played by Emmy Rossum. Man, Fiona made me feel *seen*. I love Fiona. And the depiction of how generational trauma affects each character differently... fantastic story telling.

Addiction is inherited. Point blank. We all might try to fight it, but that shit is in our DNA. And it sucks because not only do we have to bear and witness the pain that this disease causes our loved ones, but we also have to live it out for ourselves. And that part sucks. I thought I could handle alcohol even though it was written so clearly that genetically, I cannot. But nope, I rode that shit all the way out to damn near death. And these characters do the same.

Our parents are our first teachers. What they do sets up our initial conditioning for who we are, how we live, and what we do when times get hard. And yes, this is why most fucked up kids have fucked up parents. But remember, you are **not** your teacher. You are you. And you do not have to end up like your parents, you can learn quicker than they did.

Frank is a perfect example of alcohol winning. He is dancing with the devil — all the time. And what makes it so interesting is how aware he is of his bad decisions. He just has no interest in changing. Frank is smart. Very smart. The whole family is smart. Isn't it interesting that most addicts are?

For Frank, I think his life experiences were too painful and he just doesn't want to break the habits that help him cope. That's how it is for a lot of addicts. Some just don't want to change, and that is okay because there is nothing you can do about it. If you want to quit drinking, **you** have to do it. You are the one putting the bottle up to your mouth and swallowing, no one else, which means you need to be the one to put it down. Only **you** can end it. Frank knows this and he sure as hell pays the price. His children fucking hate him.

Frank and Lip also remind me of my mom and me in a way. We both have AUD and it connects us, but our experiences have also differed drastically. No one's journey is the same when it comes to addiction. I learned from my mother's mistakes, but I still had to learn on my own. Lip, just like me, knows that drinking has caused immense pain in his family's life and he knows that he has the same disease as his father, yet he still picks up the bottle. And it almost permanently ruins his life. Sound familiar?

Our parent's mistakes help us without realizing it sometimes. We can break down addiction if we first look at it in its true form: an inherited disease. A disease that we are born with and conditioned to feed. Lip was taught that drinking is what you do. So was I. But thankfully, a lot of us Millennial and Gen Zer's are doing a great job at breaking these generational curses, or at least taking note of them. Awarenesses is always the start.

Again, there is a spectrum with alcohol use and everyone's use varies, but it is safe to say that Frank and Lip have extreme cases of AUD. I am not saying that my family life was exactly like the Gallaghers, it is a TV show, but the tone is definitely there. Everyone grows up in different environments and develops different cues that lead them to make decisions, but damn, *Shameless* does a great job at making it relatable to those of us that struggle with addiction, family wide.

34

Side Effects of Not Drinking

It would be wrong if I did not mention some of the negative side effects of *not* drinking. In my opinion, they do not even come close to the benefits, but are still worth mentioning as they do exist.

#1 — **Boredom**

Not drinking is extremely boring *at first.* Losing the thing that makes life more "fun" and "bearable" is not an easy feat. It's like time goes slower and I am just staring at the truth — that truth being who I really am and what my life has become. Having to deal with pain, with no easy way out, is probably why most people don't quit their vices. And honestly, I get it. Facing the truth of one's life decisions is not easy, especially if there is a lot of trauma involved. But I have found beauty in the boredom... and the pain. Hobbies help. Fun easy mock-tail recipes help. Not throwing up stomach acid every morning *definitely* helps.

Quitting drinking was drastic for me in many ways, but the effects it had on my social life were the most major at first. It was hard to be around others that continued to live the same way that I had, so I chose to stay home alone instead. And to be honest, I cried a lot those first few Friday and Saturday nights watching posts of friends out at clubs having "fun." But then I would have to remind myself that those nights never ended as "fun" for me — not when I was binging. It has definitely gotten easier as time goes on, but the first year was **hard**. And I definitely still cry about it sometimes.

Social media is not great for someone trying to quit drinking. It made me feel isolated and sad. But I had to accept that I felt even more isolated and sad when I would wake up with no memory of what happened the night before. I guess we really do need to *choose our hard*. Not going out like I used to and feeling like I am constantly missing out on experiences and meeting new people sucks. When I first quit, I had to delete social media for an extended period, it was too hard to watch. Social media addiction is real and everyone around you will continue to do what they do, and *that is okay*. Choosing yourself is not easy — it's why most people don't.

Fun Fact: The definition of bored is, "feeling weary because one is unoccupied or lacks interest in one's current activity." So, if you look at boredom from a literal standpoint, you will realize that it has nothing to do with anyone else and everything to do with **you**. We are in control of our boredom and can easily find other activities, people, and interest to make alcohol sobriety more interesting. Not drinking is hard, but drinking (for some) is harder. Be easy on yourself — at least that's what I'm doing.

#2 — **Loneliness**

Not drinking is lonely. Quitting is isolating yourself in a way. Not everyone wants to be around a sober person when they are drinking, especially when that person used to be their favorite drinking buddy. This means that some invitations that used to come through might not as often anymore. It sucks, but I have learned to not take it personally because the people who don't want to be around me now aren't icing out the real me, they are icing out a version of me that no longer exists. And that I can live with.

Sometimes I really do feel like I have no friends though. I know it's not true, but I definitely have a lot less around now. It just wouldn't be the same with my old party friends. We have nothing in common unless there is a bottle in front of us and that's not *true* friendship. I prefer quality over quantity these days. And honestly, I have grown a lot in my loneliness. After that first year, my loneliness turned into solitude — and solitude I **love**.

I have made new friends since I quit that also don't drink, which has helped. It is so interesting hanging out with the "other side" when I was a part of the blackout crew for so long. It's different, but these are truly some of my most valuable relationships now. When making friends sober, you have to *actually* talk and be present. It will make you pickier with who you spend your time with. I have a good friend now who has never drank before. I repeat NEVER, not one fucking sip. My mind was blown. And she is one of the coolest girls that I know.

What I want in a friendship is different now. I also think that I have been hanging around the wrong crowds for most of my life. I have an addictive personality, which means I should limit how much time I spend around people who party with alcohol and uppers. I also prefer friends now who are capable of having raw, honest, sober conversations for hours at a time, without a "turn-on" substance. They are the most fulfilling to me.

#3 — **Being Uncomfortable**

Yes, you will need to get used to being uncomfortable — especially in environments where you used to heavily drink. I get serious social anxiety when going out to bars or clubs now. I didn't even enter one for at least a year into my sobriety. Luckily, there are a lot of non-alcoholic options for us these days, but they were not as popular during my first year in 2022. It was tough.

A good thing to also note is that some people, who you used to go out with, won't know how to communicate with this new *you*, and that might make them uncomfortable. How can you blame them? They only know how to communicate with the lower vibrational "you" that alcohol puts you at, because that's where they are. And again, this is okay. People can only meet you where they are.

I try to go out every so often now and be around the drunk crowds as it's pretty interesting from a creator's point of view, but it gets old quick. Like damn, I cannot believe people have been acting like this the entire time and I had no idea! It is a light switch, I swear. You see darkness coming out of people once they have had a few too many, and most of them don't even walk or talk right after. Let me be clear, I was one of "them" for a **very** long time, usually the worst. All my friends called me "Blackout Elli" for a reason.

The spirit of alcohol brings out the deepest insecurities and fears in humans. And sometimes, when I am around it too much, I feel like it is trying to punish me for not partaking anymore. Which is where the uncomfortableness really stems from. It's as if it's trying to attack me for not being with *it* anymore.

Alcohol is a toxic ex that always wants you back. It is persistent, it is strong, and it is tempting. However, the way to get through this is to realize that at this point, **you have won**. I have fucking won. And I will continue to be winning in this fight as long as I never have another sip. And that is enough to motivate me to never drink again.

And as a plus, I always wake up the next day feeling *amazing*.

To me, none of these are actually side-effects. They are simply changes of living a true and honest life. Every day is beautiful for me now, which is not something I could have said before. I will take these side effects over drunken conversations, nasty hangovers, and non-remembered sex any day.

Substitutions

Mocktails are a jumping industry right now and I love that for us, but they can also be expensive. I would like to share a few mocktail options that work for me *and* a budget.

I started with Diet Coke. That is truthfully what helped me quit at first. I would drink that shit for breakfast, lunch, and dinner. Once an addict always an addict, am I right? Haha. Now I treat myself to one or two a month as a "treat." Okay maybe 1-2 a week. I am trying! I just don't want to *recommend* DC to anyone because it is honestly a little addicting itself — so tread carefully, I guess.

Below are a few non-addictive and cost-effective drinks that I consume to satisfy my cravings.

1. Club Soda with lime. Classic.
2. Kava Drops (the bottle is pricey but lasts), sparkling water, and cranberry juice.
3. Kombucha in a wine glass.
4. Ginger Beer. Yum.
5. CBD waters.
6. And Diet Coke, because fuck it. Or Coke Zero. Or Diet Pepsi. I just prefer Diet Coke. Add a lime.

My favorite is #2, especially if you top it off with a fresh cut lime. Chefs kiss. Oh, and then Kombucha. I drink Kombucha all the damn time. Gives you great poops!

2025 Note: I don't use the Kava drops or drink CBD waters anymore, but they truly did help those first few years. DC and Kombucha are my top two go-to's now.

35

My First and Last AA Meeting

While I know that AA helps millions of people stay sober, I do not believe that it is for everyone... including myself. If you are an active AA attendee reading this, I truly hope to not offend you here.

I did not need AA to quit drinking. I actually never attended a meeting before I quit. The first meeting I went to was when I was over a year and a half alcohol-free, and I have still yet to be back. It just didn't feel right for *me*. My mom also always did compare it to confession at the Catholic Church, which is also *not for me*. I am by no means saying, "Fuck AA." Never. AA is awesome. How could I ever be against something that helps millions of people just like myself? What I am saying is that it is not the only option, at least not anymore.

With technology, there is endless information now about getting and staying sober at our fingertips. They even have apps that make specific plans to track sobriety. So... for those who are self-researching homebodies like me — you do not need to put yourself in a situation that makes you uncomfortable in order to get and stay sober. That's how AA made me feel... uncomfortable.

Researching and writing this book has felt like my own version of AA. It's helped me stay alcohol-free. It's forced me to continue to learn and educate myself. It's forced me to talk about my story. I didn't quit drinking the "traditional way," if that even exists. We are allowed to follow our own path and do what works best for us. And for me, writing my way through alcohol-sobriety is what saved me, not in person meetings with strangers.

I will be honest though... building "community" has been harder considering I do not like to leave my house, but that is where social media has actually helped. There are a lot of great accounts and groups supporting each other through sobriety. For me, it's still been a solo and interesting process discovering who I truly am through all of this, but I have preferred to do it alone — that is what has worked for *me*. And I just hope that whatever *this* is I am doing, also helps others. That's the goal here, to help through story. And so, I need to continue to be honest about that, and again, this is just my personal experience as a 26-year-old girl. What do I know!

The image I had of an AA meeting before attending was "old stinky men in a dark room with donuts and coffee." And when I arrived, that is exactly what I found — old stinky men in a dark room with coffee, but NO donuts. How disappointing. I love donuts. Also, no women. Given, I did go to a night meeting alone in Downtown Atlanta, so not sure what I was expecting. Okay let me dive in a little more about that night.

It was cold as fuck and I was walking around this massive church a few blocks away from my apartment for like fifteen minutes trying to find this damn meeting. Why are they so hard to find? After more searching around this church, and multiple failed attempts to enter rooms, I finally found the correct one. And when I entered it was very clear to me that I was the only set of tits in the vicinity.

I immediately felt uncomfortable. Maybe it was my social anxiety, or maybe it really was because I was the only woman. Leaving was my first thought, but I decided to stay and sat in one of the outer seats with a good view of everyone in the meeting. It was the type of crowd you would expect, and I did feel a sense of knowing and comfort with them all, but I also was overthinking about what every single person was thinking about me. Which was just fucking stupid because no one cared, as they are literally fighting for their lives. Which leads me back to... social anxiety. (And maybe a little bit of self-centeredness.) I also have a lot of trauma with drunk men. I think the combination was just too much.

I sat quietly and listened as everyone spoke, which was helpful. And even though I enjoyed parts of the meeting, I still left as quickly as possible to run home like the writing obsessed observer that I am. What I wrote that night goes as follows...

It is November 16th, 2023, and I went to my first AA meeting tonight, a year and a half after my last drink. When I walked in, I stood out like a sore thumb. The meeting was held at a church in Midtown, Atlanta and I was one of two women in the meeting (the other one was collecting attendance, so really the only one).

A few things stood out to me when listening to the meeting. First off, writing this book is the reason I have been able to stay sober. The reason I was able to get sober in the first place was finding my spirituality. It was as if everything the meeting leader was saying was exactly what I have been doing, I just had been doing it in my own kind of way.

I wish I would have gone to a meeting earlier, but I have always had a bad taste in my mouth. Turns out meetings can be very informative. I just don't feel like I belong, physically, even though I am just as much of an alcoholic as any one of those guys. I just stopped drinking earlier than most. I also watched my mom go to court mandated AA meetings so I was familiar with it in a negative way. That's not very motivating.

The leader of the meeting was cool. He said in order to be an alcoholic, alcohol has to have power over you. Well yes, that is true. He also talked about how it is a physical illness like an allergy. I liked his reference to an allergy. That's like how I say it has the vampire effect, the blood thirst. I guess another way to say that is "allergy." I like vampire blood thirst more though, but that's just me.

I wanted so badly to stand up and speak about my story, but I pussied out. I think I felt guilty because I still smoke weed, so I wasn't sure if I was even allowed to be there, and again, that is my issue with these things — feeling judged.

However, it would probably have been beneficial to have a group of people to talk to during my early stages of alcohol sobriety, but part of me thinks that I was always meant to face this journey alone. At least to this point.

Okay, this is what I would have said in the AA meeting if I had the balls to get up and talk:

"Hi, I'm Elli and I'm an alcoholic. I have been sober from alcohol since May 4th, 2022. I wanted to quit since I had my first blackout at age 14, but I still had about ten years of drinking, and hundreds of blackouts to go. Sex was a dangerous part of my addiction. There are a lot of men out there that I have slept with and I don't know their name or even what they look like. One of them could be sitting in this room for all I know. When I lived in Europe, I would wake up in some of the strangest and scariest places. I partied fucking hard. It started young, drinking liquor at 14 like it was water. All I ever wanted was the freedom of that blackout, even though it was what was killing me slowly. I hit rock bottom on my own. I also quit on my own. For myself. By myself. Drinking would have killed me. Probably from feeling too much guilt and shame. Can you die from that? Probably. Okay, the truth is, I was able to stop because I found my own version of God. It saved me and it continues to save me every day. It is a part of me that I will never let go of, not in this lifetime and hopefully not the next."

I really did want to share, but my first thought was, "Can I smoke weed and go to AA?" I don't know all the rules and I fucking hate rules. Is there a correct way to be an alcoholic? Ugh. It took time to admit that term to myself. That I was an *alcoholic*. I have always hated that term because that term took my mom away from me. It is the term that haunted me for years when I was struggling with my own disease. But after that first AA meeting, I do see more power in that term. Maybe, that is what helps people quit — a strong sense of being *something*.

As you know by now, I prefer the term AUD. But at the end of the day, I am just another grade-A alcoholic, *baby*. □

2025 Note: I ended up going back to a few AA meetings this year without working the program. Great place to meet like-minded individuals!

See? Forever *changing*.

36

Trapped In Corporate America

Jobs are like men, replaceable.

I quit my job three weeks after I quit drinking. Everything had to change. Also, I just didn't like selling basketball tickets anymore, *especially* not sober. My job with the professional basketball team involved a lot of drinking — secretly. I drank (for free) in the club sections at games and shows knowing damn well I could get fired for it. I just always knew I wanted to be the *client*, not the employee... ugh.

My job consisted of running around the courtside club damn near every night trying to manage at least ten different overpaying, ego-filled, mostly men's (ugh), *feelings.* And these feelings... were usually about **basketball**. Hello? I couldn't care fucking less about basketball! And to care enough to yell at lil ole me? Like come on man, *I can't help it that they suck!*

Please note that this is not me bashing the position or working in sports, I loved my time there and all the people I met. I just never wanted to do work like *that.* I didn't belong there. I also just don't like sports (other than Steelers football) that much and if I were to be honest, I worked all those years in the industry because I liked watching all the hot guys *playing* the sports — up close and personal. ◻

Working for the professional basketball team was a very developmental period of my life. It is where I decided I would become an actor. In early 2022, before I quit, a well-known Atlanta actress became one of my clients and we had a conversation in the courtside club one night. She told me her story about how she got her start in acting. She was a costume designer but eventually spoke up for herself that she wanted to act, and her boss (a well-known filmmaker) gave her a shot. She was in her 30's at that point and she *killed* it. Her life completely changed overnight. Fucking magic. Also, there was something else about her that made me do a double take and it's actually one of the first things that I noticed about her. That is, when she sat down to talk to me in the club, her friend she was with said, "X, you want a drink?" and she ever so kindly replied, "No, thank you." Y'all, the courtside club has an all-inclusive bar with every liquor option possible — an alcoholics' paradise. But nope, she refused, just as so many women I looked up to at that point have.

That was the moment that truly inspired me to start taking my dreams seriously. I saw something that I wanted more than anything — to be a **sober** actress. And the only way for me to get there was to give up everything that I knew. My whole life revolved around alcohol for as long as I could remember, so to quit, I needed to be free from all of the controllers that surrounded me. When I left the courtside club that night, I was changed. I was going to act. And a few months later... I quit drinking. I will never forget what X taught me that night and I don't think she even knows the impact she had. She was beyond kind. She is a *true* star and her light shined bright on me.

However, I couldn't run away from a day job just yet. Bitch gotta pay her bills! I thought about going into more detail about all the jobs that followed this one, but nah, that's not fun. And this book is about drinking.

Fun fact: I met one of my best friends, Kinah Jones, while working for the professional basketball team. I was drunk as hell in the courtside club one night with the Married Man when we met. That night is a major reason why I am so grateful for that job. Kinah and I had some wild times over the next few months during and after games. She is one of my greatest friends today and we have been through a lot. I wouldn't take back anything from those days.

Okay, back to the topic at hand. I've been professionally motivated since I was a young girl, which most likely stems from how my father raised us. I got my first job when I was 14. Working hard is in my DNA, whether I like it or not. I am programmed to work, and I have always wanted to create a happy life for myself. However, with age, I am learning that Corporate America is not the only way to attain money. For some, including myself, working in corporate is a **dream blocker**. I have never been afraid to quit a job. I have actually quit almost every job I have ever had. So yes, I am one of those Gen-Z'ers. *Sorry not sorry.*

Quitting is powerful.

Seriously, we need to remove the fear behind leaving something that is no longer serving us. This can be a partner, a job, a living situation, or... maybe drinking. We attach this idea that doing "well" is sustaining and keeping things going. Like job tenure, or "But we've been together for 5 years how could we just let all that go!" or "I've been drinking like this since I was 14, no way I can change!" That is living in fear, not freedom. Quitting something that is no longer good for you is the peak of living well and choosing yourself.

Life taught me young that stability can only come from within. My life never felt stable as a kid. So, maybe that plays a part in why quitting and leaving comes more naturally to me, but still... you can have this too.

There is a lot of pressure around drinking alcohol when it comes to fitting in, but this is especially present in the corporate world, at least from my personal experience.

Drinking in the workplace is a whole other beast for an alcoholic. Why? Because you can get in a lot of trouble, like **a lot** of trouble. Say you blackout at the corporate Christmas party and say something you shouldn't, well, just know that you are probably fucked. Why? Because your employer will never see you as a victim regarding alcohol use, *no no no*. Now you are a "company liability" and they will most likely fire you. Merry Christmas!

Right after graduation, I was set to start my first "adult job" at a staffing agency in Denver. A good friend of mine from college got the same role, but my start date was a few weeks before hers. I was already working there when she had her "new hire happy hour" with a Senior Account Executive to get to know her better — *aka* judge her and make sure she is a fit before she starts. My friend struggled with AUD just like me, however at this time it was not something we were willing, or able, to admit. The transition from graduation to being a real adult is confusing. And so, my friend had a few too many cocktails at this "happy hour" and she ended up blacking out and not remembering everything that she said. Also, this "happy hour" was with one of the attractive male sales reps at the company, which I believe was a total set up. Sounds like a hot date to me! Not even a day later, the Sales Manager called her and cancelled her start date. I mean sure, she should not have blacked out and started talking about the things that she did, but the bitch is smart and would have done great at the job — without alcohol. That's the catch with these jobs, especially sales — they push so much alcohol on you and then fire you for drinking. WTF.

In my opinion, it was fucked up that they even made her meet, BEFORE GETTING PAID. I felt really bad for her because I knew she was just like me and turned into someone else when she drank. She had an alcoholic monster too. But these sales companies are vicious and don't care. This one was also filled with mostly frat-like guys, so considering that my friend is a hot little blonde with big beautiful fake tits... come on.

Fortunately, I was always pretty sneaky and smooth with my drinking at jobs. Not everyone knew the extent of my issues with alcohol. I have always tried to keep my private life *private* when it comes to the workplace. Which makes it even funnier that I am putting all this shit in a book. Most people that know me will be pretty shocked when reading this, especially past employers.

The world makes alcoholism easy to hide. We use alcohol as a way to "fit in" and interact with other people. And the truth is that "happy hours" have the power to ruin careers, which ends up not being so *happy*. But we are told that it's how you get promoted. This idea is so fucking odd and it makes it really hard for those struggling with AUD to survive in the workplace.

Also, it is scary as hell to get your first "corporate" job, because it's like overnight you are now spending half of your life in a cold room with strangers

— and don't forget the mandatory heels and pencil skirts! Oh, wait, also don't forget that these *strangers* suddenly have total control over whether you can pay your bills! AND (drum roll please) they might even make you stay AFTER paid work hours to force-feed you alcohol. Woo!

Sure, they say it is to "get to know you better," but really, we all know that they are either testing to see if you will say something stupid *or* they are grooming you for an extramarital affair. *Fun right?* I mean hey, as long as Karen in HR is buying the margaritas, I should go get drunk and feel "comfortable" enough to tell her something just to end up fired on Monday! Boo-yah!

I somehow surpassed fucking up my job at a happy hour, but alcohol still took its toll on me in the workplace. I was always hungover or "sick" at work. It was at its worst in college when I was working as a recruiting intern for the football team. I would sleep through work missing complete shifts, or be throwing up in the office bathroom, sometimes sleeping in there too. Not my brightest days.

I understand that I do things "differently," and that it's a blessing shit has worked out for me the way it has. I know that's not the case for everyone. The corporate workplace is hard. And really, the way that some of these companies are run is criminal. So, to all my fellow AUD'ers, please be careful, and **don't** blackout in front of the people that sign your checks. And also, most importantly, **don't** let your day job take you away from living a creative life.

37

I DIDN'T EVEN GET TO SEE LEBRON JAMES

In 2020, I won a company raffle with the professional basketball team for two tickets to the NBA All-Star Game under COVID-19 regulations. A few friends of mine from the job also won tickets, so my ex and I made plans to host the pregame at our place. One of my work friends brought a bottle of Hennessy and it is safe to say that we went *in*. I knew that smoking and drinking in massive consumptions before going to my place of work was not smart, but I didn't fucking care. I just wanted to get lit and see Lebron James do some tricks!

We got absolutely obliterated (speaking for myself) and somehow made it to the arena. The funny thing is that I never knew how drunk I was until it was too late. I ran into a celebrity, who is a part owner for the team, but *more importantly* married to one of my favorite female CEO's who I had a massive business crush on at the time. My drunk ass decided it was a good idea to aggressively run up to him with my business card and say, "Hey X, please give this to your wife!" He looked at me like I was crazy. Which was fair, considering this was one of the first in-person events after months of social distancing, and his kids were with him. *Apparently,* I just shoved it at him and then ran away. Nice.

Quickly following that, I went to the giftshop and took a selfie with my ex. I had a massive beer in the picture, a beer that I do not remember finishing, because after that selfie, it was lights out... no one's home. The event had not even started. Still to this day, I remember absolutely nothing from the entire event. Not getting to the seats. Not being in the seats. Not leaving the seats. Not seeing any player… no tricks. And to top it all off, my boss's tickets were *apparently* seated right behind me… not a great combination.

The next morning when I woke up, confused as always, I saw that I had a concerned text from my friend who I went to the game with. She was like "Hey, (Boss's Name) came up to me during the game and was wondering what was wrong with you. I was like trying to help you but Kareem (my ex) was there and I just didn't really know what to do." Guys, I was passed out in my seat the entire time. And remember, it wasn't a packed arena. During COVID-19 regulations, it was like two occupied seats and then eight empty seats in-between each pair to abide with the 6-foot "social distancing" rule. I was there, but not *there*, for 3+ hours, with zero memory of the event. I remember fucking nothing. And the saddest part about all of this is that it was "normal" for me. I quietly woke up with a broken heart because *I didn't even get to see LeBron James.*

Later that morning, I received a text from my boss needing to "talk" (yikes). I was like, *oh god, here we go again*. This was not the first time drinking had gotten me in trouble at work. Luckily, I have never been a screaming, yelling, nor loud drunk — which most likely contributed to me never getting fired over drinking. I was more so a *sleeping in public* drunk. Think… lifeless. A sad and depressed zombie drunk, which honestly might be worse than being loud and screaming. My kind of blackout drunk makes people feel bad for you. It's also the kind that is much easier to take advantage of… you know how that goes.

My boss let me off with a warning of "inappropriate work behavior." I had a few more bad drinking episodes after that on the job, but none that I was caught for. And luckily, I quit drinking before I could sabotage what really mattered to me — my dreams of acting and writing.

Over the years, I have drunk slept walked through various cool events, shows, and *apparently* work events. Remembering nothing, always relying on others to tell me what I "did." I was sick. I was sad. I didn't want to be here. Alcoholism is not always "aggressive drunks" or "wildness," sometimes it is just drinking to the point where your mind can turn off because that is how horrible it is to be in it. Fortunately, now, I love being in my head. Well, sometimes. It still drives me crazy, but at least now I am clear about what I am doing. I will never be that drunk zombie in public ever again.

And the next time that I am at the NBA All-Star Game, I will remember it. And for Lebron... I am sure you sparkled that day.

38

Plant Medicine

I smoke weed. Or as I now like to call it... *plant medicine.*

During my first few months of alcohol sobriety, I had at least two blunts a day... sometimes three. *Fat* blunts. Okay, I know this isn't something to brag about. But hey, it was better than two blunts *and* two bottles of wine per day. Growth comes in waves y'all... baby steps.

If you are starting to judge, let's take a pause. I never said I was 100% sober. And quite frankly, I don't like people who judge weed smokers. Like shut up. And leave us alone. Pot heads hurt no one. I wish I was just a pot head from the beginning. Literally 95% of my trauma would not have happened.

Weed helps me. Alcohol was my vice. And when I quit alcohol, I also quit all recreational drugs other than weed & shrooms, which I consider to both be plant medicine. Quitting stimulants is something I am very proud of. They were a trigger of mine for blacking out. However, this book would have definitely been done by now if I were still taking Adderall or Vyvanse, lol. Just saying.

But like I say... choose your hard.

I look at plant medicine as a tool, not an escape. The goal is to use it with intention. Weed and shrooms are sacred to me — they help me work through internal exploration and enhance sensory imaging while I am at home creating. My best experiences with plant medicine are always alone. I love being high and alone. That might sound dark to some, but it's actually the opposite for me.

However, sometimes I do ask myself, "Am I a drug addict?"

I think the answer to that is that once you're an addict, you're always an addict. And that can be a hard pill to swallow for some. Because it's like you quit one thing and then boom... here's another! But by the age of 26 I am able to say that I quit alcohol, stimulants, and loveless sex — so it's a win in my book. I don't plan on being a pot head my whole life, but right now I am. It helps. And if I am going to be addicted to something... *let it be ganja!*

Fun fact: The first joint I smoked was with my younger stepbrother. I was fourteen at the time which would have made him twelve... and it was his weed. Classic.

2025 Note: I was, in fact, turning into a drug addict. Happy to be totally sober now, but don't regret any of it.

39

My Last Blackout

It was the end of April 2022 when I had my last and final blackout. My 25th birthday had just passed and a dear friend of mine, my Taurus sister, was having her annual birthday party a few days after mine. At this point, I had been on the edge of wanting to quit, but habits are strong and so I decided to go to the party and drink. I also ended up taking an Adderall halfway through the pregame, which always sent me straight to *blackout city*. The pregame was great, as they usually were, but then we went to a local club in Atlanta.

By the time we got to the club, I was already close to a blackout. Also worth noting, by this time I had developed a very strong level of confidence, which turned me into a bit of a savage when drinking. The last thing I remember was being at the bar and not having any cash on me, so I lined up a few guys and had them all buy me drinks. I was always pretty good at getting other people to buy me drinks, especially the more that I drank. The last thing I remember is slurping down a double rum and coke and then... waking up in my bed. No phone. Same clothes on from the night before, shoes included. I was facing the entirely wrong damn direction on my bed. At this exact moment, I remember feeling *defeated*. I was so sick and tired of waking up like this and not remembering anything. I was 25 now and I knew that I should be able to go out without blacking out every single time, but that never was the case for me. I only let myself dwell for a few minutes until, like clockwork, I popped up frantically to search for any remembrance of the night before — most importantly, my phone.

After getting up too quickly, resulting in a quick throw up, I went out to my living room and it was a mess. This was pretty usual after a night out and when I was looking around for my phone, I stumbled across a... note? Yes, there was a note sitting on my bookshelf and it said, "Please call me when you wake up, I need to make sure you are okay. – Tiffany." First thought, *who the fuck is Tiffany*? I don't know a Tiffany. Again, what the fuck Elli, you are supposed to be past this shit! And then my inner voice started saying, "but at least you are in your apartment alive, it's not so bad!" This was my usual train of thought, trying to rationalize my behaviors as "normal," but this pattern wasn't "normal" or at least not the "normal" that I wanted to be anymore.

I threw the note across the room and continued to search everywhere for my phone, but it was still nowhere in sight. So, I decided to do what I know best and open up Find My iPhone. I was a serious professional at using it by this point. I always somehow found my phone. This time the app said that it was in my apartment, but again, nowhere to be found. Fortunately, I had plans to go to a Braves game with my friend that lived upstairs, so I opened my door to head up and then, *ta-da*, my phone was face down in the stairwell. First thought, *I never take the stairs, what the fuck*. I had NO idea how it got there but I grabbed that shit and ran up to talk to her. I was so capable of operating "normally" after nights like this, aka not remembering anything. Because it was just that, *normal*, for ten years. However, the underlying guilt and anxiety were always there, continuing to compound.

After talking to my friend, I headed back downstairs to shower and get ready for the game and to my surprise, there was a voicemail on my phone from Tiffany. I pressed play and after 20 seconds I stopped it. I could not even finish — it was that bad. She must have carried me into my apartment or something because she was VERY concerned. And so, instead of calling her back and thanking her for probably saving my life, I deleted the voicemail like the little avoidant shit that I was back then. I was going to pretend like it never happened. And I prayed to never see Tiffany again.

However, the next day, she did knock on my door. I froze and thought about answering, but instead I ignored it and pretended I wasn't home. I was too embarrassed to face her. I know it was rude, but I was so scared that she saw something that I didn't want to know. I don't remember what happened that night and part of me never wants to know. And to this date, I still don't know who Tiffany is or what she looks like, and she lives in my fucking apartment. I wonder sometimes if she ever rides the elevator with me and is like, "*what the fuck is wrong with this girl.*" Little does she know; she was a savior to me. That voicemail did something to me. It scared me so much that it somehow pushed me to never do that shit again. So, thank you Tiffany. You were my last blackout saving angel.

Okay, there's a little more to this story. Apparently in the midst of my blackout, I called the guy I was dating at the time. I still have no idea what I said, but he texted me the next morning saying something like, "you scared me last night." Again, when I blackout I turn into a "zombie," like lights out, no one's home, but I am still walking and talking. It's not attractive, it's scary. And he probably saw a really terrifying version of me. I called him once I got up at my friend's apartment and truthfully, I gaslit him into thinking he was crazy to be so concerned about what he saw on that Facetime the night before, which I still have zero memory of. Poor guy, he was so sweet.

Part of me was so numb during these situations. I just went up to my friends, said fuck it, and started to get ready for the baseball game where I was 100% set on taking full advantage of the all-inclusive bar in the Braves Delta Club. Also, on nights where I did not hurt anyone, hook up with anyone (to my knowledge), or injure myself, I felt like I had a "successful night." Boy was I wrong.

This last blackout affected me different than most because once I got to the Braves game, I was physically unable to day drink like I usually did. Something about that night scared the living shit out of me. I know something bad happened. I just don't remember what. It felt dark. It still does. My friend that was out with me that night told me later on that she got me into my apartment building. So, whatever happened, happened either privately in the club or after

I entered my apartment complex. And whatever it was still haunts me to this day. This was my last blackout for a reason.

My true and **final** last straw to quit was a bit random. It was a few days after that last blackout while I was on one of my 72-hour strikes. I started the 72-hour's shortly after that Braves game, partially because of how repulsive the liquor felt going down that day, and partially because of how I felt after I had that last glass of wine at my friend's house which I spoke about earlier. Just seemed like a great time to try and quit. And fortunately, this time it stuck.

On the second morning of my 72-hour strike, I discovered an album that Jack Harlow had just released. As I was listening, because I fucking love his music, one song in particular did something to me that I can't really explain. The song is titled, "Young Harleezy." Right after I heard this following line on the track, that was it. The line was, "bottles in the section marked Fiji." Yep, that was it. That was the exact moment I decided I would never drink again. He is basically saying that he is sober now and all this bottles in the section are "marked Fiji," like he is only drinking Fiji water in the club. Genius. I still don't know why, but it gave me the last bit of confidence I needed in myself to quit. Thanks Jack.

I am not fully sure why it was this exact scenario that pushed me to the finish line, but I do think a big part of it is that I know I want a life in the public eye. And so, if Jack Harlow could quit drinking and still be a star, *why not me*? Also, by this point, my purpose in life truly felt bigger and more powerful than ever before. I was finally able to see my worth and what I truly wanted. And there was only one thing holding me back from going for it all. I knew then that to become who I am destined to be, I had to give up alcohol. And so, I finally said to myself, "me too."

I need to be clear and reiterate that it took me years to get to this point. Years of trying to quit. Years of 72-hour strikes. Years of interventions with my friends. Years of watching myself destroy my body and confidence over and over again. It is not an easy thing to give up your greatest vice, but it is absolutely 100% possible. I managed to get through that last 72-hour strike and make it permanent because I decided to finally choose myself. I chose to love myself more than I ever had before. I chose to love myself enough to throw away the *thing* I always thought I needed to be loved. I finally kicked out my abuser, alcohol.

Those ten years were hard. They were challenging. And a lot of shit happened. I am not a bad person, I never was, but I have done some bad things. I got myself into some deep shit over those ten years — deep places of unbearable, isolated pain. Every hangover was painful, more mentally than physically. However, I do not enter that place anymore.

That place is *dead*.

40

Social Media Gives Me Crippling Anxiety

"Comparison is the thief of joy."

Not sure who wrote this quote, but damn is it true. And more specifically, comparing yourself to others on social media is a tried-and-true recipe for self-esteem destruction.

Sure, my relationship with social media didn't start off strong considering the whole "Harry Harry Dicks" fiasco, but even without that I would still be fucked. We all are. And to top it off, the shit is *addicting*.

I was always jealous of people who didn't drink, but that's not all. I am also jealous of people who don't use social media. When we are jealous of something someone else is doing, it is usually a sign that there is something we, ourselves, should do to change. But this is always easier said than done, and so I still struggle daily with social media addiction.

But Elli, if you were able to put down the bottle, shouldn't you be able to put down the phone? Well, one would think. But no, this is a whole different **beast**. And what a beautiful prison Inst*gram is.

Knowing what other people are doing at all times is not natural. In the olden days, we would have to wait weeks, if not months, to get a response back from a friend or lover. But now... if they don't answer within five minutes, we are immediately checking social media to see what they are doing. Like, "How could he not text me back?!" "What is he doing?" "Who is this new bitch he is following?" "Oh my god, he watched my story but didn't text me back?! He must be cheating. Or he hates me. Now I hate me. WHAT THE FUCK."

Like I said... prison. Mental prison. If this were the 1800's, I would be happy as a clam waiting for a response, but no... now I have literal anxiety attacks.

It is natural for people to need space. It is natural for people to need time to respond. I *know* these things. But still, it's so fucking hard to control the urge to check and make assumptions of what they could be doing. When did time turn into imprisonment? How are we ever going to survive this?

It's all just too much, at least for someone like me. And to top it off, sensory overload! I delete and redownload Inst*gram at least once or twice a week (or day). If it is on my phone, I check it habitually. And then two hours have gone by. Like, what the fuck? Algorithms are *dangerous*.

The hard part about social media is that it's not all bad. It can be an amazing and powerful *tool*. Especially for someone who is trying to make it in entertainment, like me. But what's the difference between a tool and a weapon? How you use it? Maybe the only real way to manage social media addiction is with *intention*.

So, I have decided to treat social media like art. Appreciate it for a short period of time, get what I need out of it, and then walk away. Think of it like going to a museum. And people's pages are their galleries. Yes, I like this a lot more. And if I am following someone whose museum I would not pay to go to? *Unfollow.* No regrets.

I am also someone who just doesn't like everyone knowing where I am, where I am going, or what I am doing — but then I go ahead and post it. So, am I the one to blame? Is social media just a mass representation of the toxic relationship we have with ourselves? Ugh.

I think a lot about how Pete Davidson said he downloaded Inst*gram for a day and almost killed himself. I feel that. Sometimes it's like laser beams of negativity shooting into my skull saying, "You suck and you have accomplished nothing! Your acne is awful! But *hey*, here are 45 options to fix it because I heard you on the phone crying to your mom about last night. Haha, you're welcome!" *Siri?* Hello???

Help us. Help us all.

Also, as with anything I talk about in this book, not everyone has a relationship with social media like I do. Not everyone feels this way about it — just like how not everyone is an alcoholic.

I have started to put more effort into authentic connections and friendships in *real* life. I try to stay off my phone when hanging out with friends and loved ones. But honestly, this has caused me to be even more hyper aware of how much other people are on their phones. It's sad and I hope as a collective we can all work on staying off of social media when together. This is where not having it downloaded on the phone helps. I think everyone should give that a try. And books, books help. I try to read a physical book at night rather than scrolling. Again, I am not perfect and still fall victim to the occasional doom scroll, but it's the effort that counts. And these more positive habits have already begun to compound... day by day.

41

A Collection of Shorts, N'at

Time for a few short stories and *thangs,* because why the fuck not!

30 Days of Walking

Read and walk. Read and walk. Read and walk. I went on so many fucking walks my first 30 days of not drinking. Like so much walking... for hours at a time.

There was this lady in the suburb that I grew up in who we all called the "walking lady." She was as thin as a rail, crispy tan, and about 40-50 years old. All she did was walk around the local neighborhoods and... talk... to herself. All day. Just walking and talking. I always figured she had some mental illness or something, but honestly, I don't know anymore. When I think back on it, she might have just been fighting something. And I think she was fighting whatever that was... by walking.

I turned into my own version of the walking lady those first 30 days. Well, minus the talking to myself, or at least not *as much* of the talking. And I swear to God, every time that I went on one of those monstrous walks, I always thought about the walking lady. I just kept thinking, like damn... she was really onto something. And shit, I can't believe I was judging her. This walking shit works! Sure, I have always been a walker, but this was a different level. It was a part-time job. I walked my way through anger, grief, guilt, shame, abandonment, confusion, hurt, tears, screams, laughter, pain... and just like clockwork, by the end of every walk, I always felt like I had fought through some internal battle. Like I had gone to war and defeated something. Something that was deep. And it felt... freeing. So, I became addicted to it. *Obviously.*

Quick note: I am so sorry if you are reading this and you can't walk. I don't really know what to say here... maybe just wheel around? Crawl? Scoot?

Reading also helped me during those first 30 days. Not this non-fiction bullshit (my book included) — no. I am talking about some crazy ass romantic-horror murder shit, or maybe some sexy Fae war fiction? It needs to be something that takes you into a different world and keeps you off your phone.

And grit. That's what really got me through those first 30 days. *Muthafuckin'* grit.

My First Tattoo

It was the morning of my seventeenth birthday and my mom called me to tell me that she was picking me up from my dad's because she had a "surprise" for me. She didn't tell me where we were going, which always made me a bit nervous. After about twenty minutes of driving, she pulled into a random parking lot near the city — a parking lot that just so happened to be in front of a tattoo shop. I was confused at first, but then it set in... my surprise was that I was getting my first tattoo.

At this time, my father was strongly against tattoos. This really summarizes my childhood, that my mom would take me to go do something knowing damn well if my dad found out, we would have both been in trouble. My mom has always been a risk taker, and so if she said *fuck it*, so did I.

We walked into the shop and she looked at me and said, "So what do you want to get!?" Well, I had no idea what I wanted to get because I did not expect to permanently ink my body for the first time that day. She reminded me that her first tattoo is a sun on her groin and how it always reminds her that "the sun is always shining," especially on her "hoo-ha!" So, I did what I knew best — I copied my mom.

Her sun tattoo was always more than just "the sun is always shining." It also represents how badly the women in our bloodline need the sun to feel happiness. We always feel our best while at the beach, so, really, I set that as the reasoning for my new sun tattoo. I also just needed some fucking light in my life back then.

The artist let me draw the exact sun shape I wanted, and after he cleaned it up a bit, I showed him where to place it. I needed it low enough so you could never see it in a bikini, even a tiny one. He said to come back in two hours and then he would be ready for us.

My mom and I went down the street to Starbucks, another usual for us (also another place my father despises), and waited for the appointment. I was nervous, but she told me it wouldn't even hurt and that I would be okay. But still... I was terrified.

We made it back to the shop and once I was all settled in the chair, I pulled down my underwear. I swear I screamed when he first pulled out the tattooing gun. I wanted to back out but my mom was right there holding my hand telling me it would be okay, and so I let that random man aim his little gun straight at my vagina because that's what tough bitches do! And again, I *really* needed that sunshine.

Now and forever, the sun is always shinning on me *baby*.

After the appointment, I knew that my biggest mission in life moving forward was to hide the tattoo from my dad, because he most certainly would not have let me go to college in Colorado if he found out. Fast forward to today and he still has no idea about it. Dad, if you're reading (hopefully not), *sorry*. But also, blame your ex-wife!

Killian was the first person I showed my new tattoo to. We had plans to go to the John Mayer concert that night (his idea, not mine) and I whipped out my new pelvis bling like it was the winning golden fucking ticket. He just looked at it and laughed. He knew it was crazy but would never judge me. He was my favorite guy back then for a reason.

I enjoy the pain of tattoos and that day started my journey with them. It is a form of art and fortunately, for my generation, most of us have them. My second tattoo was one that I got with Fiona during our first week of college... and it's the Coors Light mountains on my left rib cage.

Lmao, fuck.

Leprechauns and Jamaica

Ever since I was a little girl, I've seen *things*.

The first time was when I saw a leprechaun in kindergarten. I kid you fucking not. It was Saint Patrick's Day, and I swear on my life that I saw that little green man speed across the floor. I was only five years old, but that exact moment was when I first believed in extraneous beings. *I saw him*.

Then there was the first darker "being" that I saw. I was nine years old and we were in Jamaica for my dad and stepmom's wedding anniversary.

Fun fact: They were married in Jamaica when I was seven, but we won a free trip back because on their wedding night a rabid jumping squirrel got into their room and tried to attack them. Okay, back to the story.

We were at Ricks Café (where I was cliff jumping for the first time) when I saw *her*. If you have ever seen the movie *The Ring*, think Samara, or at least her twin look-alike. Her figure had been haunting me in my dreams for months prior to that trip, but this was when I first saw her *in real life*. I am not sure why she haunted me for so long, but after seeing her there, it was as if I had no option other than to *accept* her. I remember standing in my oversized dripping wet t-shirt (directly following the cliff jumping) and I just froze. I couldn't stop staring at her. I told my family about how scared I was, but no one understood what was going on and just considered me "crazy." And so, I laid awake at night for weeks with nothing but her on my mind. The nightmares eventually stopped. I like to believe she was my "darkness," and I had to accept her as part of myself in order to be free of the fear from her. I had to accept a lot of dark and scary things at a young age. So, maybe she was just a figment of my imagination that I created to cope through my trauma.

But I don't actually believe that — I know what I saw. The leprechaun too!

Victoria's Secret Fashion Show

One night during my junior year of college, I went over to two of my best girlfriend's apartment. They had also invited over two of our close guy friends, who just so happened to bring over at least four different stimulants. So, the five of us decided to do as many of thus stimulants as we could within the span of the 2018 Victoria's Secret Fashion Show. We snorted Vyvanse, Adderall, Coke, a little bit of Molly, and took at least seven shots of Burnette's each. Lines, shots, lines, shots, lines, lines, more lines, and shots.

We were lit.

And I can full heartedly say that I do not remember a second of that fashion show — it was all lights.

After a few hours of who knows what, I finally got my shit together and headed back to my house. However, *you guessed it,* I was locked out. It was late and a Tuesday, so my roommates were not answering my numerous calls and knocks. My ass then decided it was a good idea to call one of the football players that I had a *massive* crush on and ask him to come pick me up and stay at his house.

Within fifteen minutes he picked me up and of course, we had sex.

I remember feeling extra shitty after this night because I was so fucked up, but not in a blacked-out way, more so in a coked out hungover way. Scary. And this was a guy that was getting ready to head to the NFL draft. Our lives at this time could not have been more different... and it made me sick.

Sure, I had a "crush" on him, but I don't think I ever really wanted him — I wanted his *life.* I wanted to be the star player. I wanted to be on my way to make millions of dollars in the spotlight. I wanted to be in his shoes, not his bed. But nope, I was the drugged-out *slut* instead.

To this day I cannot watch the Victoria's Secret Show without laughing. That is not the Elli that I know anymore.

Miss Spider-Man

One of my best friends, Hannah, is *very fun.* I could and want to write a lot about her, but I am going to keep it to just this story.

After the bars one night our junior year (and a few too many Vegas bombs later) Hannah and I arrived back to my house and of course — we were locked out. Instead of being normal human beings, we decided it was a good idea to have Hannah scale my six-bedroom house in the dead ass of winter, break through my upstairs window, and then come back down and let me in. And so, Hannah, being the badass that she is, fully scaled the side of my massive icy house on the main strip of campus, broke through my second-floor window, and successfully came down to let me in. Superhero level shit. The house was old — not an easy fortress to climb. I still don't know how she did it. And the worst part of it all is that I missed it. How? Well, I missed it because I was fucking blacked out, and truthfully, the only reason either of us know what happened is because one of my roommates was also locked out and watched all of this conspire.

When Hannah came down to let me in, I was passed out... in the snow. What a mess. There but never *there*. Missing "Miss Spider-Man" will always be one of my biggest regrets.

Kylie

In early 2024, I was casted to play a dead girl named Kylie that killed herself in a drunk driving accident. Go figure, right?

Basically, this short film follows the lead character, played by one of my dear friends Emilia Torello, who is mourning the loss of my character. About a week after the accident, I suddenly appear in the lead's apartment and am haunting her looking.... spooky. While my dialogue was slim, the role quickly became very personal and serious to me. And that's because of how much I could relate to *Kylie.*

I had always refused to drive drunk because of what I saw DUI's put my mom through, but life happens, and with age I started to fall into the same habits.

There was one night during the winter of 2021 when I was driving home drunk and believe that I saw my life flash before my eyes. I think about this night often. Thinking about what would have happened if I didn't make it home safe. Well, I probably wouldn't have ever known because I would be dead. It was really close. I downed at least half a bottle of tequila that night.

All I remember is having one eye open and one eye shut, steering damn near blind, going up 85 in Atlanta. I felt my body fighting a blackout mid-driving and almost totaled completely into my exit ramp. I am not proud of this moment; I am actually scared of it. Addiction is scary — it will have you doing shit you never thought you would do.

And so, with this character, I was able to fully tap into the mindset of if I had died that night and how I would feel. Challenging, yes, but also healing. I wrote a journal from Kylie's point of view. She struggled with alcoholism, just like me. And depression. She didn't want to be dead. That was clear. I played her as if she was in purgatory finding out she is dead and having to watch her best friend mourn. I looked so scary y'all. Kylie couldn't move, because she is dead, so it was a lot of internal dialogue. In her head she was like, "BITCH! WTF! Why am I dead?" and "I was literally just out having fun and met that new guy and yeah *maybe* I am a little depressed and have a drinking problem, but WTF I don't deserve to die!"

That's how Kylie felt. But it's also how I believe I would have felt. I would have been so pissed if I had died that day. I have never wanted to be dead, but I did so much dumb shit that brought me close. Too many times. And I am so grateful every day to not have lost my life to drinking.

Also, this story is just an example of why I act. Turning pain into magic. Hurt into art. Fear into freedom. Getting your power back is the most influential thing you can do for yourself and others. So, why the fuck not?

Dear Buns

Buns, Bubba, Pookie, Bous-yons, Oreo, and Chicken,

Hi baby you look sooooooo cute right now laying over there on your favorite corner of the carpet. I love you soooooo much!!! You are so perfect!!!

I need to write a thank you letter to you even though you will never be able to read nor comprehend it.... or could you.... I definitely feel like you know how to talk and just haven't shown me yet. I can hear you telepathically — but I am so ready for those vocals. I just want to know what your voice sounds like. I feel like it is a combination of Ariana Grande, Miley Cyrus, and Jennifer Coolidge. Or maybe Morgan Freeman and you are secretly a boy!!

Nah, you have a hoo-ha. But if you want to identify as a man that is okay! I am not judging you. I love you no matter what. To me, you are perfect. But you have told me you identify as "dog" ... so, I guess it doesn't matter what gender you are? Okay, before I take this too far down a road that's unnecessary, I think you have a voice like Mariah Carey, I know it. You can def sing.

Okay okay, on a serious note, thank you for being my emotional support being these past four years. I am so sorry that I fed you so much wine and beer our first two years together, but I do believe it is what made you extra magical. We just opened up those little brain receptors in your little head young! And now it's impossible to go back! Still, I am sorry. I know it wasn't right to turn you into a little alcoholic too. That was fucked up of me.

I made you an Inst*gram so that we could make you famous like Taylor Swifts cat but then I got off Inst*gram to finish this book (and really for my mental health). Inst*gram is so bad for us Buns. We have addiction issues outside of just alcohol, but nevertheless, day by day. Once I sell a million copies of this book, we will hire someone to run your social media account because the world deserves to see you. You are too perfect to not be seen. You deserve it!

Thank you for existing. You are my first born. We have a long way to go but I am so grateful for how far we have come.

P.S. I apologize for how many stepdads you have had. I promise that one will stick soon.

I love you,
Mother

42

How To Not Become a Millionaire

It is known by many that I am a true businesswoman at heart. I love business. Why? Well, I love professionally arguing with people about why they should give me all their money. Haha! Okay, I'm kidding (kind of). But really, I want to make my mark in business. I also crave nothing more than some good ole' financial freedom. So, after I moved to Atlanta and COVID-19 hit in early 2020, I got involved with a few people who told me that they could, in fact, teach me to make a lot of money — 25k per month to be exact. And all I had to do was pay $200 a month for a forex subscription and then convince everyone I know to pay for the same monthly subscription, but this time, using *my link*.

Like, "Wow! Brilliant! Of course, this is going to work and I going to be rich by the end of the month!"

I was so fucking naïve.

And this forex *team* (*cough cough* pyramid scheme *cough cough*) is what started a long pattern of getting fucking scammed — and sometimes, *innocently*, trying to get everyone I know to follow suit.

And then there was the $5,000 water machine I was told to buy because it would "make me rich." And since I was desperate as fuck because of the Forex losses (yes, I lost money, never gained), I fell for it. And yes, the same guy who brought me onto his "forex team" was the same guy that convinced me to purchase the $5,000 water machine. Go figure, right?

I am so grateful to not be 23 anymore.

I was told constantly in these pyramid schemes that they don't let just "anybody on their team" and that working with them "will make me rich." HA. Let me be clear, I asked these people all the time if they were running pyramid schemes, and they always said no. I was also usually drunk or high as fuck while having these conversations and agreeing to be a part of the "team." I remember I received one of my promotions with the professional basketball team while I was filming a video for the water pyramid scheme and both of the "leaders" didn't even congratulate me. They honestly told me I should quit my job. I wish I knew to trust my gut back then as much as I do now. But all of it was so complicated for me because the guy leading all these schemes was also a good friend of my ex's... who I just so happened to be living with during the time... in his house. And so that made things extra *complicated*. It also made me trust him a lot more than I ever should have.

Okay funny story, I once got so blackout drunk at one of the forex "retreats" and, *apparently,* I stood up in front of everyone and said some rude shit to the "billionaire" they had staying at the cabin with us. I don't even remember what I said, I just think deep down I knew that all the shit going on was *bullshit*. I was so desperate to make something of myself. Turns out, these people did see my worth, they just had no fucking idea what to do with it. And they also had no fucking idea how to make any real money. Period.

If you know me, you know I am a great saleswoman, so of course, I tried to convince my entire network to join the pyramid scheme. I am so sorry if you were a victim of my efforts. I was desperate, y'all. And plus, these guys were my "friends." My friends who I technically paid. Like... what the fuck, Elli? I honestly almost quit my job with the professional basketball team for these fools. The buffoonery. *Fun fact*: it was only ever MEN leading these efforts. Makes sense now.

Pyramid scheming men, my least fucking favorite.

So here is my current list of thoughts I came up with on *How To Not Become A Millionaire*. I know these things because I did in fact do them and have not become a millionaire — yet! And the men who told me that I should do these things are, in fact, also still not millionaires. These were tough lessons, very young. Thousands of dollars worth of lessons. And then I had an even *tougher* lesson in 2023, which I will get to. I am still only human, and we all make mistakes. I just wish I didn't have to make so many that involved money.

How To Not Become A Millionaire:

1. AI Forex. AI Forex. AI Forex. AI Forex. Run. Run. Run. RUN.

2. Calling everyone you know and telling them to join your AI Forex team. (I am so sorry again if you got one of those heinous messages I was sending out.)

3. Buying a $5,000 water machine because some guy you met at an AI Forex meeting convinces you that it prevents cancer and that if you buy it, you can now also sell them and become a millionaire... as long as you use his link! Fucking run.

4. Hearing out any offer from any random man that you just met who asks you to be the "face of his company" ... RUN.

5. Meeting with another random man at Starbucks who also asks you to be the CEO of his radio company because none of his family members want to take it over... I still can't believe this happened. And that I actually considered it. RUN.

6. Considering taking out a *** loan with information from the same guy who sold you on the AI Forex and water scam because he knows it's "legal" and you are "entitled" to it. FUCK. RUN. Please. Thank God I didn't go through with that one.

7. Not listening to your parents when they tell you that you are involved in something dangerous and that these "businesses" are in fact PYRAMID SCHEMES. Run!

8. Lastly, giving a man that you met online an obscene amount of money because he says that he will help you "triple it" through his marketing company. This is my worst mistake yet. Please... RUN.

Gosh, I am stressed now just thinking about all the shit I believed... and did. The cool thing is though, once I cut these people and their "business ideas" out of my life, I ended up making my first six-figures with the professional basketball team by the age of 24. So, sometimes the day job *is* worth keeping for a little.

Disclaimer: I am sure that there are some decent forex traders and water machine sellers out there, but when it feels too easy, *something is wrong*. Money is not always easy to make. You have to work for it and *that is okay*. These get rich quick schemes are dangerous and will leave you with nothing but debt and regret. So please, be careful out there.

Okay, time for the final scamming boss I had to face, and unfortunately, this took place when I was 26 years old. Would have thought I learned my lesson by this point...

He Gave Me Acne — July 2024

I met the devil in the shape of a 6'4" handsome man with a leased-out Maybach.

And he gave me acne.

Okay, I knew something was off the entire time. My stomach and brain, they knew — as well as almost every single person in my life. They all told me to run. But my heart and vagina did not want to listen. No, no, no. We believed he was a good man and that he loved us.

HA.

Turns out he was a scammer. Certified Scammer. He got me and my business partner for $15,000 to help build our "business model" with his "marketing agency." God, he was good. Or was I just naïve?

I am 27 now. I am learning. And technically I was 26 when I signed his shitty J*tForm contract. My tech girl says I should have known right then and there. Guess you really don't know 'til ya know?

What I do know is that guy sucks. He is a lying piece of shit. He even lied about his age! Like dude, it is 2024, my super-secret investigator (my friend in LA) just sent me your file and it says that you were actually born in 1985 — like EW. Who lies about their age these days!? Scammers.

He told me he was 36. Probably so he could be "10 years older than me," just like my business would be making "10k a month," and how he would send me "10k and a trip." Ugh.

Pathological.

I should have known when one of his first messages to me was, "We can cuddle naked?" Like nice Elli... nice.

But he had a Lamborghini in his profile pic!

Fuck Elli, how could you be so naïve. They are not even his cars.

I definitely should have known after he pulled his dick out during our first time meeting, without me asking him, on MY couch, in MY apartment. He was forceful. But attractive. And I wanted him. But not like how he wanted me. He didn't want to be with me... he wanted to *have* me.

I should have had enough self-worth to tell him to leave.

The thing is, I did. I told him more than once to stop coming over. He never listened. One morning, after I specifically told him not to come over, I went down to my car to go to my 7am barre class and he was asleep in "his" Maybach. Next to my car. Passed out in the same outfit I had seen him in earlier that week.

Red flag much?

Are you homeless if you're living in a Maybach?

Oh girl, oh girl, what have you gotten yourself into.

A mental chokehold. That's what this was. I knew it was wrong. My therapist told me. She knew it. But I didn't listen — I went with him. My vagina can be a powerful bitch when she wants to be.

Am I sick?

Maybe.

What I definitely am is another $15,000 in debt because of another broke ass man. He's ugly too. Well, when you first meet him, he's good looking, but then once like thirty seconds passes and he opens his dumb ass mouth — ugly. And you just want him to shut the fuck up. He is so disrespectful. He is ugly on the inside.

He does have good dick though.

And good dick is a prison.

Scammed by another man — in Atlanta fucking Georgia. I wish I could say this was my first time getting scammed... it's not. But it will be the last.

A criminal who thinks he is a businessman.

Was my self-worth really that low to allow this man so close?

Or was he just a really good scammer?

If I have learned anything it is that one does not need an STD to have a dirty dick. His dick was dirty on the inside. His entire being is.

He gave me acne!

43

WHO AM I NOW?

The more time that I have put between myself and alcohol, the more I realize that space creates a new existence.

Think about it, the more space you put between an ex-relationship or ex-job or ex-*habit*, the easier it gets every day to be without, and to move on. Why is that? Well, the space between then and now expands, and it creates a new existence, a new feeling, a new sense of being.

The more space and time that I put between myself and my abuser, alcohol, the stronger my reason for quitting becomes. I no longer live in the past. I exist in the *now.* My life feels new. I no longer live in regret of my past actions and experiences because I forgave myself — I am different now. I am *new.* And this *new* Elli cannot be touched like she used to be. Never.

And really, was there ever anything for me to forgive? Wasn't I just growing? This is not and never was a "poor me" story.

I am not a victim, not anymore.

In a world filled with AI, we need imperfection in our arts.

Who Am I?

I am not who I was when I first started this book, that's for damn sure. I have grown. Writing all your trauma out with the intent to share it with the world is definitely a vulnerable experience — in the greatest way possible.

There is one major realization I had while nearing the end of my writing and that is: ***I already am who I am meant to be***.

What I mean is that I no longer am striving to "become" something or someone else, I just *am*. Sure, I still have to work my ass off day in and day out to obtain my goals. But now, when doing so, there is no one else that I feel like I am needing to become. I am not trying to escape or run away from my life anymore. I am settled. I am here. I am at home.

And that is not something I could say three years ago.

I no longer feel trapped and stuck in patterns with no end in sight. I no longer live to please others. I no longer look in the mirror and *hate* what I see. My daily depression no longer stems from a place of shame or guilt. It stems from more livable things, like credit card debt and asshole boys.

Writing and acting fuel me. I want to do these things. I want to be alive. I want to be in my body. I want to work. I want to live my life. And through it all, I found passion and a purpose that fuels me more than any bottle of liquor ever could.

Is this freedom? Or is my brain just finally working correctly? And with all this time and knowledge... who am I now? Well, let me tell you...

Acne

For twenty-five years I had flawless skin — literally perfect. Not a pimple or scratch in sight. It was honestly at its peak when I was binge drinking Pineapple Burnette's every day and chasing it down with string cheese, knowing damn well I was allergic to both. But still... perfect baby butter skin. Then, once I quit drinking, and am now years into being dairy free... I have acne. All over my face. What the fuck?

It all started when I turned twenty-six, which was around the time that my mom was diagnosed with Non-Hodgkin's Lymphoma. I think it was a combination of the stress around that, being sober (alcohol-free), shitty men, job losses, and really just all the years of suppressed trauma coming to the surface without the crutch of alcohol. And I guess it all decided to come through my face.

Acne is such a battle. It is embarrassing and makes me want to not leave my house, which honestly, I already don't really like doing. It's just awful. I also now feel immense sympathy and sadness for everyone in my life who had acne when I was younger and I acted like it wasn't bad. Because it is bad. It feels bad, and I wish I had more sympathy for my friends back then. Acne never looks as bad as it feels, which *I* am now being told on a daily basis, but still, it's *uncontrollable.* Like a wildfire out of nowhere. And gosh, there are so many "cures" and "products" and "specialist." Like fuck, just the stress of trying to figure out which products to use is giving me even more acne! And then there's the money aspect... oh the amount of money that I am now spending on trying to fight this red rage on my face! Ugh.

Maybe my body really is just adjusting to finally *feeling* all my feelings. And all thus feelings are just purging out of my face. Yeah, that makes sense.

Laura Chinn's Memoir, *Acne*, has helped me in my battle with acne. She reveals a lot of truth through her story, and it helped me get to the root of mine. First, stress. Too much stress. Stress = Acne. But she also brought a feeling to my attention I hadn't quite considered yet, and that is *anger.* I am angry. I am so fucking angry underneath it all. Teenage Elli is ANGRY.

So, maybe this acne is telling me that it's time to finally deal with this side of my trauma. I need to feel the anger. I need to feel the hurt. I need to purge more than just the acne out of my body; I need to purge these emotions. And as challenging as it is, **the only way out is through**.

2025 Note: I am three years sober now while completing final edits for this book and my acne is clearing up. Trust the process. It's also just funny because the internet literally says to give up alcohol and dairy to help acne, but I did that and then got it for the first time. Fighting acne is an individual battle. I have been told by countless dermatologist that I need to take a massive amount of medicine, but I always said *no.* I knew I could clear it naturally — and I am.

Also, I moved to California and am at the beach almost every day now, so that definitely helps too. Follow your dreams y'all, *follow your dreams.* Oh, and weed. I had to quit the weed. Smoking copious amounts of weed gave me acne. Ugh.

OCD

I have OCD. I didn't really know it until I quit drinking, but ya... I have that shit. Which honestly just makes a lot of fucking sense. Like, I am happy about knowing it because now I can accept it and move on with my life. I am just *different.* Maybe even... special.

I tried to run away from my compulsions, but I can't. I tried to drink them away, but I couldn't. And all the effort I put in trying to rid those feelings only ever made them worse. It wasn't until I finally accepted it that I felt the peace and freedom I had been craving. I find peace in the chaos of my brain now, because it makes me unique. And I wouldn't want anyone else's brain now but my own.

I wouldn't say that my OCD is chronic, but it is present. My apartment has to look the same every night. I try to sit there in bed and not move the one remote that I know is out of place in the living room, but I can't help it. I have to put it back in place. Kinda like how I had to have the next drink. It was obsessive. Compulsive. *Obsessive Compulsive Disorder.* Also, peeing. I have to go pee three times before bed every night. It's annoying, and maybe I can figure this one out one day, but as of now I just fucking do it because once I do, I feel so much better. I also struggle with cheek biting and picking of the face. Ugh. Never ending work.

To be totally honest though, the majority of my OCD presents itself as intrusive thoughts.

Lexapro helps. And now that I have lived alone for a while, it's easier to manage. But that's the thing, I live alone, and I don't always want to. It's just hard to live with other people because I get so mad when they don't keep things the way I want. It makes me *angry*, which is not fair for anyone. For so long I've let small things drive me crazy. But now, since I am more aware of why certain things make me feel a certain way, it's getting easier to manage. I know I can live with people again one day, they just need to respect me, vice-versa. I am not crazy. It's just OCD!

Since accepting this pattern in my behaviors, I am able to work on better communication tactics. I also choose to spend and share space with people that respect me and understand that I am not perfect or necessarily "normal," and that's working so far. Age helps too. I am becoming more accepting of myself and others. But first and foremost, it all starts with awareness. Those without self-awareness just don't have a place in my life anymore.

Also, OCD is great (for some) because you will never be late — at least not on purpose. I think in segments of time, with everything. However, if things are not going according to **my** time frame, issues will arise. So, there we have it folks, some more shit I still need to work on. Ugh, being amazing is *so hard*.

I'll ever be "normal." But really, is anyone? I work hard now to try and not take my issues out on other people. But again, I am not perfect. None of us are.

2025 Note: Okay, I was wrong. I have hyperactive ADHD with OCD *ticks*. Finally got a doctor to rightfully diagnose me. Makes so much more sense.

Bulldozer Elli

I am a bulldozer. Sometimes in a good way, sometimes not so much.

And alcohol made this bulldozer *out of control*.

When drinking, I had no power over the steering and speed it was going. I also had no control over what direction it was going or when it would stop. I just knew it was *going*. Taking me to countless bars that I would never remember, taking countless shots that I would never taste, and having endless conversations that I would never recall. Sure, the bulldozer sometimes took me to great places, but also sometimes to the brinks of hell.

I never wanted this "thing" to be a part of my personality, but it is. So now, I am learning to use its power for good, not bad. Plus, since I quit drinking, I at least have some sense of control over it. I am aware of its power and am learning to drive it. I am also learning that sometimes it just needs to be fucking parked. Again, *still learning.*

My bulldozer now looks more like saying too much when I should just shut the fuck up. I *promise* that I'm just trying to help people, but it doesn't always come off like that. It actually comes off as being judgmental, cruel, and makes people question what they can say around me. I don't like making people feel like that. I just can't fucking help it sometimes. That is where the OCD starts to creep in too. I guess what I am saying is that just because I quit drinking and wrote a book does not mean I have everything figured out. I am just like any other random person of the street — lost and confused.

Maybe my intrusive thoughts are the bulldozer. That would make sense.

Just as I had to learn to quit drinking, I have to learn how to control some of these other destructive traits. And I do apologize if my bulldozer has ever personally affected you. It can be a powerful bitch.

"Sober" and *Single*

I am single and in my mid to late 20's — yes. And going out is hard so I prefer to stay my ass inside. Bars and clubs are difficult to be in when everyone else is drinking. People change once alcohol enters their system. They get too touchy. They say things they would never say without their liquid confidence. And it feels odd to be around, but not on, that frequency anymore. It's uncomfortable.

So, I read a lot. I love to read. It is one of my favorite things to do. When I was drinking, I could not read. I would attempt to start my nightly reading with a glass of wine, but that slowly turned into a bottle, and then the words would blend together. Now, I get to spend a lot of my nights reading. I can sit down and read a whole book front to back again, something I used to do often when I was younger. I recently crushed Julia Fox's memoir in one sitting... it was *excellence*.

I dance now too. I love to dance. It's how I let it all out. No one has seen me do it though, and I plan to keep it that way... at least for now. I know I could do it on camera. So, I guess the world is going to see it one way or another. What I really want is to be able to go out to clubs and bars and dance freely, but I just feel so awkward and stuck. I hope with time that this changes and I learn how to just not give a fuck anymore.

At one point in my life, I had purple hair and two horribly infected nose piercings. You would think I was someone who didn't give a fuck, but honestly, I gave more fucks than ever during that time. I was a mess. Sure, my life is still messy now, but in a way that I like. It's not like it was when I was drinking. It's manageable. I am a healthy wild woman. A single and ready to mingle *wild woman*.

The Ending Is Just a New Beginning

I understand that this book may rub some people the wrong way and that there will be a select few who will judge me, specifically regarding my past sexual experiences. The thing is, I really don't care. Well, I do, for like a second, and then I remember that people who have opinions regarding someone else's sex life are fucking weird. And then I remember that it is actually pretty badass of me to share my full truth — there is a lot of power in vulnerability.

Healing does not happen overnight, but a change of mind can.

I was relieved when I finally decided to not care what people thought about this book, and that's because I know it's going to help others more than it will offend. Also, other women before me have sprinted so I could run with my story. And shit, maybe I am sprinting too. Maybe we all are just fucking sprinting because this shame that we as women face is so fucking horrible at times that it makes us just want to explode. That's what this book is — me exploding.

And don't even get me started again on the topic of "body count." I repeat: *Does rape count towards a body count? You wanna talk about that on your stupid little podcast? Does that make your tiny dick stand up?*

Realness overrules judgement any day.

I know who I am now and I know what I stand for. My body is finally *mine* again. I forgave myself for those dark nights. Awareness is the key, and what matters is what you do with that awareness. I am just a human with a past. We all have one. And having sex (safely) is fun! Just do it with someone that you love, or at least *like*. Also, I have been called a whore since I was 15, so it really doesn't faze me much anymore.

Something else that all of this has taught me is that you only truly know that change is possible once you do it. Some people never even try, which is why they aren't able to fully understand how someone can. But listen, I changed. Massively. So, you can too. DNA and patterns are repairable.

Writing this book was one of the hardest things I have ever done. Having to relive certain memories and pain *over and over and over* again, in more detail each time, was hard. Especially the stories. But I needed this book. I needed it in order to stay sober from alcohol. Also, I needed to heal through these memories. This book has saved me, even during the countless hours crying over my keyboard, it has truly saved me. I have saved myself.

And hey, we are only as sick as our secrets, right?

It has taken me time to figure out who I am without alcohol, and turns out, I am just **me**. Thats it. I am still wild and say outlandish things. I still speak my mind and tell the truth. I am real and authentic and I literally don't know how to lie unless I am in front of a camera. I am just Elli. Brutally honest, Elli. But now, I am Elli without the cloud. Without the weight that I carried for so long while keeping up with my disease. And without all the psychotic shit I would do while blacked out. I am free from my captor, *alcohol*. Writing is my escape now, not Al-Kuhl.

My whole reasoning for this book can really be simplified down to this: If someone would have handed me this book at the age of 18, it would have changed my life. Or at least implemented the idea that *I* can change my life. And that is enough for me to push print.

Grateful For Not Being Alone

None of this would have been possible without all the love and support I receive from the people in my life. I am very fortunate to have a circle who truly sees and cares about me. People that I can trust with my whole heart. We all need this. We need community. You may go faster alone, but we will always go farther together.

I don't think I would have had the balls to pursue my dreams without my friends. I don't think I would have had the balls to do a lot of the things without them. Friendship, specifically *friend family*, is what fuels me and keeps me alive. They check me where needed. They ground me. They fuel me. Without solid (specifically female) friendship, I would be lifeless. And I truly mean that.

Then there is my mom. My mom is one of my best friends now. I tell her everything, maybe even a little too much. But that's the best kept secret of growing up with your mom rather than being raised by her — a built-in best friend who you just so happen to have the same genes as. She never judges me for what I say or do, but she does keep it real. She is my mirror, and that's a very valuable thing.

And so, as we close this story I still have to ask: *Who Am I Now?*

Well. It's simple.

I am Elli Rose *fucking* Cikovic.

44

WHY I QUIT (2025)

As I write this, I am over three years alcohol-free, living in Southern California, and finishing the final editing of this book. But there has been something stopping me. Something holding me back. Something telling me I am not done yet... until now.

As of June 2025, I have officially entered the realm of "sober." Basically, I no longer smoke weed or take shrooms — something that I talked so proudly about before. It is not my goal now to share in detail why I have decided to take these steps other than to say that I have. I will share my why eventually, just not in this book. This book is about alcohol and it needs to stay true to my first two years being *alcohol-free*. And during those two years, I smoked a lot of weed and took plenty of shrooms.

I don't regret anything because I was doing my best, I still am doing my best. However, my crutches are gone now. And the funny thing that I've realized is... I was always able to stand on my own. I don't need a fucking crutch, at least not anymore. I am enough. And life became so much more beautiful once I realized that fighting addiction is easier than living in it. Sure, both are still hard — you just have to choose your hard.

And so, as I leave you now, I want to reiterate how strongly I feel about this next statement:

You can wake up any day and choose to change, or you can wake up every day and choose to stay the same.

We all have free-will, but I chose change. I continue to choose change. And who knows, maybe after all of this it will be time for me to put away the antidepressants too. Because honestly, part of me feels like the extent of my chemical imbalance stems from addiction and unresolved trauma. But for now... baby steps.

I love you all. Thank you for reading my story. And don't forget...

FUCK ALCOHOL.

Acknowledgements

While every word (and error) of this book remains my own, I truly need to thank a few people who helped me along the way.

An immense thank you to one of my dearest friends, **Fiona Rae Anderson**, for hand-editing my final drafts over the last year and giving me the perspective I needed to finish this out. I am forever grateful for you and your time. Ah, and for the most *perfect* author photograph — what a talented woman you are. I love you, my moon!

My mother, **Liz Antonio** — *oh,* my sweet mother. Thank you for reading through my manuscript and not wanting to murder me (lol)! And for fact-checking my ass where it was necessary. Then of course, thank you for your blessing to share so much about our life. I am beyond proud of *us*. I love you with all my heart.

Kinah Jones... everyone needs a Kinah Jones in their life. Thank you for reading all my unhinged essays early on in the process and telling me how amazing you thought they were. You helped me find a confidence in my voice that I didn't even know existed. I love you more than words can say.

And finally, to everyone who has read thus far — THANK YOU! This book has been my heart and soul for almost four years now and I am just grateful people wanted to read it. Love you all too.

Okay, that's officially a wrap. □

xoxo, Elli Rose

References

Abbott, P. (Creator). (2004–2021). *Shameless* [TV series]. Showtime. (cited on p. 205)

Barrymore, D. (n.d.). [Quote on sobriety]. (cited on p. 29)

Chinn, L. (2022). *Acne: A memoir*. Little, Brown and Company. (cited on p. 256)

Clear, J. (2018). *Atomic habits: An easy & proven way to build good habits and break bad ones*. Avery. (cited on pp. 46, 199)

Coelho, P. (1993). *The alchemist*. HarperOne. (cited on p. 53)

Gilbert, E. (2015). *Big magic: Creative living beyond fear*. Riverhead Books. (cited on p. 47)

Michael A. Singer. (2007). *The untethered soul: The journey beyond yourself.* New Harbinger Publications. (cited on p. 188)

Mayo Clinic. (2022, October 19). *Alcohol use disorder*. Mayo Foundation for Medical Education and Research. (cited on p. 74)

National Institute on Alcohol Abuse and Alcoholism. (2023, October). *Alcohol use disorder: A medical condition characterized by an impaired ability to stop or control alcohol use despite adverse consequences*. U.S. Department of Health and Human Services, National Institutes of Health. (cited on p. 72)

Sullivan, J. (2021). *Bodies* [Song]. On *Heaux Tales*. RCA Records. (cited on p. 7)

The Vampire Diaries. (2009–2017). The CW Television Network. (cited on p. 34)

"Young Harleezy." (2011). On *Section.80* [Album]. Top Dawg Entertainment. (cited on p. 232)

Hanna Dylan [@hanna_dylan_]. (n.d.). Instagram. (cited on p. 115)

Essay: Depression, 2012

Annes, J. (n.d.). *Nothing but respect*. Understanding Depression & Suicide. Retrieved October 2, 2012, from

CAMH: The causes of depression. (n.d.). *Depressive illness: An informative guide*. Pan American Health Organization. Retrieved October 2, 2012, from

DePaulo, J. R., & Horvitz, L. A. (2002). *Understanding depression: What we know and what you can do about it*. Wiley.

Dixit, J. (2009, March/April). You're driving me crazy. *Psychology Today*.

Gillham, O. (2009, October 6). Depression is the most common cause of suicide. *Tulsa World*. SIRS Issues Researcher.

JianLi, W., & Pattern, S. B. (2002). The moderating effects of coping strategies on major depression in the general population. *Canadian Journal of Psychiatry, 47*(2), 167.

Maj, M., & Sartorius, N. (1999). *Depressive disorders*. Wiley.

Maloney, M., & Kranz, R. (1991). *Straight talk about anxiety and depression*. Library of Congress Cataloging-in-Publication Data.

Nordenberg, L. (1998, July/August). Dealing with the depths of depression. *FDA Consumer*, 27–31.

Roleff, T. L. (2000). *Teen suicide*. Greenhaven Press.

Schieble, S. (1999, August 21–22). Suffering in silence: More than a state of mind. *Patriot Ledger* (Quincy, MA), 1+. SIRS Issues Researcher.

Whitehead, T. (n.d.). A depression recovery story. *HealthyPlace: Trusted Mental Health Information*. Retrieved October 8, 2012, from

Made in the USA
Coppell, TX
09 March 2026

73416363R00163